D0082981

COMPARATIVE RELIGION

COMPARATIVE RELIGION

BY

GEOFFREY PARRINDER

Reader in the Comparative Study of Religions in the University of London

GREENWOOD PRESS, PUBLISHERS
WESTPORT, CONNECTICUT

Library of Congress Cataloging in Publication Data

Parrinder, Edward Geoffrey.
Comparative religion.

Reprint of the ed. published by Allen & Unwin, London.
Includes index.
1. Religions. I. Title.
BL80.2.P34 1975 291 73-19116
ISBN 0-8371-7301-9

Reprinted in 1975 by Greenwood Press, Inc.
51 Riverside Avenue, Westport, CT 06880

Library of Congress catalog card number 73-19116
ISBN 0-8371-7301-9

Printed in the United States of America

10 9 8 7 6 5 4 3 2

CONTENTS

CHAPTER I

COMPARATIVE RELIGION

What is Comparative Religion? It is a name that has gained currency during the last hundred years, with the growth of knowledge in the West of the religions of Asia, and with the development of the sciences of anthropology and sociology. Yet with all the great names that have been associated with this study, on historical, social, linguistic and philosophical lines, it is often suspected as seeking to merge all religions into one to produce 'comparatively religious' people, or by revealing the origins of religion trying to discredit more refined forms of religious life.

There are two well-known books entitled *Comparative Religion*. The first by Professor E. O. James of London, the doyen of comparative religion in this country, appeared in 1942 and set out to provide 'An Introductory and Historical Study'. James discusses the opinion of Huxley and Tylor that the minds of men being everywhere similar will tend to produce like ideas, and also the claims of historians and diffusionists that similarities of religion are due rather to intercourse between the races. With his vast knowledge of anthropology and archaeology he steers a middle course in discussing origins and magic. But he does not confine himself to the primitive and goes on to consider oriental theism and concepts of prayer, sacrament and immortality.

Four years later A. C. Bouquet of Cambridge took the same title to make 'a survey and comparison of the great religions of the world'. He also started from religious origins and worked his way up through polytheism to Indian, Chinese and Semitic religions, ending up with mysticism. Bouquet took religions and cultures in turn, rather than comparing rituals and concepts as James had done.

In 1958 a different approach again was adopted by Professor R. C. Zaehner in *At Sundry Times*. Zaehner followed the example of Humpty-Dumpty to make a word, here Comparative Religion, mean just what he chose. 'The question is which is to be master—that's all.' He asserted, with some justice, that too often students of comparative religion have concentrated on primitive or animistic religion. Whereas the great historical religions are of far more importance, in extent and influence, both in relation to Christianity and in their own right as systems of faith. Comparative religion 'has paid too little attention to the great religions of the world other than Christianity; yet these, despite the missionary zeal of the Christian Churches, still maintain their vigour and have resolutely refused to disappear. It is these religions in their relationship to Christianity that I propose to study.'[1]

All these books, and many others like them, plunge into their subjects and speedily get immersed in the great mass of material that is available. The present book seeks to ask the questions preliminary to such study. What is Comparative Religion? What are its reasons, attitudes, implications and tasks? What viewpoints does it need to criticize? How far can it judge of truth and error? Can it speak to those who are engaged in propaganda or plead for tolerance? Is syncretism possible, or are religions complementary to one another? How far have its problems been changed in view of the resurgence and reformation of religions today?

Some of these are questions of method, others of theology. Some of them are addressed to Christians, others to rationalists, Muslims or Hindus. Since the majority, though not I hope all, of my readers will belong to the West the questions are particularly concerned with attitudes that have been or are still adopted there. I cannot pretend to have asked all the questions that can arise in this vital subject, or to have answered all the ones tackled completely or with entire satisfaction. Often the answer given or suggested raises further questions. But in the main, it seems to me, these are questions that are being asked today, and that theologians often shirk. If, like the elephant's child, I have asked too many questions and am liable to get my nose pulled, I can only hope that someone better qualified will rise to the challenge, and give more relevant answers.

The very name Comparative Religion has been criticized

1 p. 11.

as unsatisfactory. It is sometimes called 'the Comparative Study of Religions' to be more precise; or simply 'the Study of Religions' to avoid comparison. To call it 'the History of Religions' is also popular, though this title suggests a study of the past only. It is symptomatic of a confused state of affairs that learned journals often have articles on the title and methods of the subject: religionswissenschaft, religionsgeschichte, the phenomenology of religion, and so on. It used to be said that sociologists spent much time discussing methods and nomenclature, in default of a subject. The subject of religion is obviously there, one of the greatest human concerns, but the problem is how to approach it. For the present Comparative Religion is a handy title and it may well be that use will establish what is convenient.

But is comparison of religions a proper study at all? Indeed is it possible? Are not the religions of East and West as different as oil and water and similarly unable to mix? The problems of judgement will be dealt with in a later chapter, as will the question of syncretism. Here it must be asserted, and this also will be developed later, that the fact of the modern confrontation of religions must be taken seriously. Comparison does not necessarily imply mingling, but study.

It may also be maintained that no comparison is possible between religions, because each is a whole that has its own standards, and embodies a religious life appropriate to a particular culture. Some would maintain that no comparisons are valid, even between peas in a pod. But peas can in fact be compared, for size, colour, position, and so on. Few cultures in the past, and none today, have been so isolated that they had no means of communication. The fact of communication is vital, and it should be possible for a believer within a system to speak of his faith in terms that some others can understand. This is possible at least between related religions, such as Judaism and Islam, or Hinduism and Buddhism. It should be possible on a wider scale today. Even very different churches, e.g. Orthodox and Quaker, have entered into discussions in recent years, so that they understand each other better even if they are not converted to each other's point of view.

Comparison, however, to be justified seriously, must not

imply judgement and still less depreciation of any faith. Huston Smith, in one of the most remarkable attempts to expound religions from the inside, has said, 'This is not a book on comparative religions in the sense of speaking of their comparative worth. Comparisons among things men hold dear always tend to be odious, those among religions most odious of all. Hence there is no assumption in this book either that one religion is or is not superior to others. Comparative religion which takes such questions for its concern usually degenerates into competitive religion.'[2]

This may surprise those whose main interest in religion comes from a missionary motive, to gain as much knowledge as possible so as to discover the weak points and undermine the religion studied. But a little reflection should show that a completely unbiased study is essential if the heart of the religion is to be unveiled, for religion is the dearest of human concerns and men will not reveal the secrets of their faith to the critical outsider, so that the propagandist can hardly have an inside knowledge of another faith. Nor can another religion be understood without complete sympathy. Perhaps there is a place for assessing the comparative worth of religions. But that is the task of apologetic theology in each religion, and it is not attempted in this book.

In trying to estimate the value of a religion one is influenced, unduly for or against, by the religion that has surrounded him from childhood, so that an objective judgement is impossible. And if the convert from another religion is asked to pronounce upon it, only too often he is so shrill in his criticism that it is unreliable. Those who speak to us, as they should, from within a faith will naturally try to show what it means to them and why it continues to hold their allegiance.

Perhaps, one day, it may be possible to make critical appraisals of doctrines between representatives of different religions. This is an exceedingly delicate task and in the past has scarcely been attempted. If doctrines of other religions have been criticized it has been in the absence of their own supporters, and often done as if they were deaf or did not count. Weak jokes were made, if not violent denunciations, about

[2] *The Religions of Man* (Mentor Books, 1959) p. 15.

the queer beliefs of other people, because everyone knew that the speaker did not hold these superstitions himself. As agnostic anthropologists have spoken of religion in general, so Christians have tended to speak lightly of other religions. But a great feature of today is that all the world listens. A speech made in London may be heard in Cairo, and a paper printed in New York will soon find readers in Tokyo.

If the day comes when we can speak to each other in charity, we may be able to discuss our differences in urbanity and sympathy. The Muslim may be able to ask the Christian whether the term Father is not too anthropomorphic when used of God, and both may ask the Buddhist whether in truth all suffering is caused by desire. Such dialogue has hardly begun, but progress towards it may be seen in the work of the Continuing Committee on Muslim-Christian Co-operation and the discussions it has stimulated. A new attitude, recognizing a new class of readers, is observable in such books as W. M. Watt's *Muhammad at Mecca*. At the outset he says, 'This book will be considered by at least three classes of readers: those who are concerned with the subject as historians, and those who approach it primarily as Muslims or Christians.' It is perhaps the first time that a Christian scholar has reckoned with a Muslim audience, and to show his sensitivity he continues, 'in order to avoid deciding whether the Qur'ān is or is not the Word of God, I have refrained from using the expressions "God says" and "Muhammad says" when referring to the Qur'ān, and have simply said, "the Qur'ān says." '[3] The next step is perhaps to have a book on Islam or Christianity written jointly by a Muslim and a Christian. K. W. Morgan has begun this by compiling anthologies of Islam, Hinduism and Buddhism with panels of contributors all of whom are members of the faith they describe.[4] But deeper comparison and criticism would come from partners whose religion was different yet who worked together and described the same faith through

[3] p.x. W. C. Smith has also aimed at these three classes, scholars, Muslim and Christian believers, in his *Islam in Modern History* (Princeton 1957), and he thought out every word in the light of these three traditions.
[4] *The Religion of the Hindus* (1953), *The Path of the Buddha* (1956), *Islam—The Straight Path* (New York, 1958).

different eyes, while each checked by the other for inaccuracies and unfairness.

It is important to criticize the indiscriminate way in which comparisons of religions are often made. There are many popular books, and publications of works by theosophical and similar societies, that make far too easy equations of religions and beliefs that have little in common. All kinds of monotheisms, for example, may be lumped together, from Judaism to Shinto, though Yahweh may have little concord with Amaterasu. Heaven is often forcibly paralleled with nirvāna and prayer with yoga. Especially in studies of mysticism are loose comparisons made so that one almost despairs of objective study.

Unhappily Comparative Religion suffers almost as much from its friends as from its opponents. It tends to attract the cranky and the lunatic fringe, no doubt because they are the very people who need a richer and wider religious experience than is provided by the formality of their own creed. There are classic examples of this. The poet Shelley was expelled from the university of Oxford for atheism, yet he was attracted by Indian pantheism, and in *Adonais* advanced even further towards faith in personal immortality.

Friends of comparative religion are dangerous if they lack discrimination in their study. The eccentric often does not, and may be unable to, distinguish between resemblances and differences. 'When one tries to discount one's special emotional feeling for one's ancestral religion, one is in danger of leaning over backwards and going to the other extreme of rejecting one's own religion rather violently and admiring other religions rather uncritically just because of one's having such intimate acquaintance with them.'[5] If there are resemblances between religions, and valuable common insights, there are no less important differences, both of tradition and cultural setting. And it is here that the theologian and the sociologist rightly cavil.

Yet valuable comparisons and evaluations can be made. In fact they are made, by all kinds of people. The important thing is to see that they are rightly made, and critically ap-

[5] A. Toynbee, *Christianity among the Religions of the World*, (Oxford, 1958), p. 101.

praised. Perhaps the most shining examples of the best kind of comparison are in the works of Rudolf Otto. First he wrote of *India's Religion of Grace and Christianity compared and contrasted*. In this he not only differentiates the mysticism of unity (*advaita*) in India from the experience of grace in the religion of devotion (*bhakti*), but he also brings out the distinctive elements in Christian mysticism and particularly the humanity of Christ and the reality of the Cross which are its essential marks. Then in *Mysticism East and West, a comparative analysis of the nature of mysticism*, Otto compares and contrasts the teachings of Eckhart and Shankara. Yet in an interesting appendix he writes of deep calling unto deep, and the mutual intertwining of the 'two ways' of mysticism. The mystic mingles what to the theologian are distinct apprehensions.

The comparative study of religions, then, can be practised, and religion is such an important and universal phenomenon that it deserves serious attention. Yet after the interest in primitive or curious phenomena in the past many scholars and politicians today, and they are oddly at one in this, act as if religions do not matter. If the churches and their missions often had an arrogant attitude to the religions of Asia regarding them as hopelessly in the wrong, the modern attitude of the secular world is just as arrogant, regarding them as unimportant. Asian religions are often thought of as past superstitions, hindrances to progress, and their religious and philosophical classics, at least as profound as Greek philosophy, are totally ignored. This is true of political, ecclesiastical, or university circles.

When R. C. Zaehner was appointed to the Spalding Chair of Eastern Religions and Ethics at Oxford, he complained in his inaugural lecture, *Foolishness to the Greeks*, that he would have no regular lectures to give or students to attend them. No doubt this was pleasant enough in one way, and he was able to devote himself to the research and writing from which a larger audience has benefited. But it is a strange reflection on a great university that it had no room in its curricula for one of the most important of all studies. The theological schools were too intent on their own dogmatic courses to pay any attention to other religions. And the Oriental Faculty was so concerned with linguistics that comparative religion was not even provided for as an optional special subject.

Few other English universities do better. Only at Manchester, London, Durham and Leeds is there any provision for the study of any but the Christian religion. There are a few special lectureships, such as the Wilde at Oxford and the Jordan in London, where small groups of post-graduates may attend a voluntary course. In the other twenty or so English universities there is no provision at all for the comparative study of religions. Yet religion is one of the subjects that has the greatest literature, the oldest history and the most widespread importance for mankind. Vast sums are available for the sciences, less for the arts, yet even social studies and theology are thought to be necessary to a modern university. But among the humanities, surely the thoughts and beliefs of men are just as significant subjects for study as psychology or social organization.

The power of ideologies is now realized, and it is folly to neglect the most powerful of all. Comparative religion is studied much more attentively on the continent, in Germany, Holland and France, and in America. But England lags behind and, afraid of new ideas, buries its head in dogmatic theology or linguistics. It is comparable to the situation of Sanskrit only a few years ago, when there were only four teachers of Sanskrit in this country, after nearly two hundred years of our Indian empire, while Germany had twenty. Sanskrit is much better represented here now, but in this language as in other oriental studies, the texts are studied for grammatical interest mainly, and although they are nearly all religious texts from the classics of the East the contents are not taught for their religious value.

More than the theologians the sociologists and anthropologists are prepared to study religious beliefs. This interest goes back to Huxley who regarded the study of the belief in a spirit world as held by primitive peoples as legitimately coming within the province of anthropology. He observed that 'the characteristics of the gods in Tongan theology are exactly those of men whose shape they are pleased to possess, only they have more intelligence and greater power.' He noted also that religious beliefs provide a sanction for conduct, as when 'the majority of mankind may find the practice of morality made easier by the use of theological symbols'. Following Huxley the social scientists have not neglected the study of religion, but have regarded it as necessary to an understanding of human society. What the theologians neglected was, partly, honoured by the social scientists. However, it was a dubious compliment, for they were prepared to regard it all as projection, the work of men's hands or the symbol of their repressed desires. And it has been maintained that the most subtle foe of religion today is not the physicist or chemist, who may often be a practising Christian, but the anthropologist, who very rarely is.

Evans-Pritchard, professor of social anthropology at Oxford, has recently made slashing attacks upon his fellows for their religious agnosticism. Speaking on religion and the anthropologist he declares that practically all social anthropologists have been agnostics. From the utilitarians and evolutionists of the last century down to today they have studied religion, in its primitive forms and as under a microscope, but they did not believe a word of it themselves. How then could they understand it, for religion is not a thing, to be coldly analysed, but a faith of persons?

Some modification of the agnostic attitude of anthropologists may be seen in the writings of Raymond Firth. He speaks of the changed climate of opinion since Huxley's day, 'the open acceptance of non-rational and irrational alongside rational components in the data of human personality', and 'the development among anthropologists of a more sympathetic attitude towards religious material in the societies they study'. This might be a backhanded compliment, for theologians and philosophers of religion would maintain that they are indeed concerned with the rational side of man. But Firth goes on to say that 'we can no longer afford to neglect the more professional theoretical analyses of religion . . . by psychologists, historians, philosophers, theologians, and other students of comparative religion'.[6]

[6] *Problem and Assumption in an Anthropological Study of Religion*, (Huxley Memorial Lecture 1959).

Firth has written chiefly about primitive religion, in the Pacific Islands, and has taken part in many rituals that he describes with great sympathy. He speaks of the 'As-If' attitude that anthropologists adopt of accepting at face value the phenomena of the religion they study. He was not asked what he himself believed, and if occasionally questions were put to him about the spirits 'the enquiry was to get my opinion, not to test my allegiance. In this sense primitive religions have no dogma'.

But other religions have dogma and plenty of it. And here a more telling criticism of anthropological method is that it has concentrated on primitive religion to the virtual exclusion of what are commonly called the 'higher religions'. Beliefs of illiterate peoples, in Australia, Asia or Africa, have been the subject of innumerable monographs. But of the great historical and scriptural religions little study has been made. Yet these are the faiths that present themselves today with great challenge to the West. If anything has been written on Hindu, Buddhist, or Muslim (or in one prominent case Roman Catholic) religion, it is from the bottom upwards, the ignorant faith of villagers, that again may be dismissed as superstitious and not as challenging to thought. The priest instructed in his religion, the scripture with its antiquity, the philosophy with its reasonings, these have been left fearfully aside.

Most of the religions of illiterate or animistic peoples are dying before the onslaught of modern civilization. Here the anthropologist almost becomes an archaeologist, and often prefers what he believes to be the 'untouched' village to the modern town. Christianity and Islam between them are sweeping millions of animistic Africans and Asians into their fold, as Christianity did in America. No doubt many old practices will linger long, as they did in Europe, but to understand the dominant religion its leaders and scriptures must be studied. This demands hard study, no doubt, with perhaps the necessity of learning a classical scriptural language, but unless that is done anthropology cannot claim to study any but the lower levels of religion. Firth is welcome in insisting that 'we are no longer content with the older positivist approach'. We must go further, and let religions speak at their highest level and by their most thoughtful representatives if they are to be considered fairly. They must be studied from without and also expounded to us from within. As a Muslim claims in translating the Qur'ān, 'It may reasonably be claimed that no Holy Scripture can be fairly presented by one who disbelieves its inspiration and its message.'[7]

At least as much as, and perhaps more than, other studies Comparative Religion demands a sympathetic spirit. For if 'empathy' is required of an anthropologist to gain the confidence of a tribe, and of a psychologist to persuade a patient to talk freely, even more does the comparative study of religions demand complete charity, tolerance and understanding. These explosive religious ideas have generated such heat in the past, that we can understand modern nervousness in touching them again. Yet they are neglected at our peril.

Above all because comparative religion deals with the faith of persons, beliefs which men hold as dear as life itself and for which countless men have died, must the fullest sympathy and understanding be ready. That is why an approach through worship is often the most helpful, for here more than in the study of history and philosophy, do the actions of men reveal their feelings.[8] The sociologists, Radcliffe-Brown and others, have well understood this; perhaps they have over-stressed the significance of ritual as against belief, but at least they have brought out its vital importance.

Huston Smith opens his study of *The Religions of Man* with a picture of men at prayer, in different lands and varying traditions. 'From mud huts in Africa to igloos in Labrador Christians are kneeling today to receive the elements of the Holy Eucharist.' At the same hours a Muslim friend in Istanbul 'is praying today, five times as he prostrates himself towards Mecca'. Swami Rāmakrishna in a tiny house by the Ganges will not speak today, observing a vow of devotional silence. And in Burma Prime Minister U Nu 'from four to six this morning, before the world broke in

[7] M. Pickthall, *The Meaning of the Glorious Koran* (Allen & Unwin 1930), p. vii.
[8] I have tried to approach this side of religion in my book, *Worship in the World's Religions.*

upon him, was alone with the eternal in the privacy of the Buddhist shrine that adjoins his house in Rangoon'. And away in Kyoto, Zen monks sit cross-legged and immovable as they seek to plumb the Buddha-nature at the centre of their being.[9]

Such an understanding of men at prayer, men and women with faiths that direct their lives and those of millions of others, is essential to beginning the comparative study of religions. This is not an impersonal investigation of an 'it', religion under a microscope, or an examination of a negligible superstition doomed to disappear. It is a study not merely of external rites and scriptures, but of people with inner hopes and faith.

Within each religious field there are particular problems that need to be faced before we can proceed far. This is especially so in the Semitic religions, which have been dogmatic ideologies, but it is not absent from Indian religions also. Some of these problems are perhaps chiefly of internal, apologetic and missionary concern. But they affect the attitude taken to other religions, in study and in life, and they must be faced. Some attempt to do this will be made in the ensuing pages. It is not a grateful task to pose awkward questions, but those who are concerned with the religious state of the world must not shrink from facing them and seeking at least partial solutions.

[9] p. 11.

CHAPTER 2

THE CONFRONTATION OF RELIGIONS

The religions of the world face a completely new situation today. Never before this century have they been in such close contact as they are now. The 'one world' in which we live, with its close communications, makes nonsense of religious isolation. Whether it is agreeable or not, the fact is that men can and do now compare religious ideas one with another and mix them together. This presents a challenge and a crisis to all traditional forms of theology.

The challenge is acute for the Semitic or Western religions, Christianity, Judaism and Islam. They have been accustomed to think of themselves as supreme, in religion and culture, possessing the highest truths and the oldest and best philosophy. Many histories of philosophy, or of other aspects of culture, consider only European forms as if they were the only ones that mattered. Even Bertrand Russell who agrees that our culture must be defective as long as it is purely European, says that philosophy began in Greece in the sixth century B.C. Yet some of the greatest Indian philosophers, whose works are still studied and expounded, lived centuries before that.

We have been accustomed to speak of the rest of the world, say India or China, as isolated, until our explorations in the sixteenth century and colonization in the nineteenth. In fact it is the West that has been isolated. India has long been the meeting-place for all the great religions. Christianity appeared there in the early centuries and the Syrian church has persisted along the Malabar coast. Islam came to India, with the image-breaking intolerance of Semitic ideology, and still holds millions of Indians in its fold. Buddhism arose as an Indian heresy, prospered for a thousand years or so and then left to take Indian religion and culture to the rest of Asia. So that the confrontation of religions today is but an acceleration in India of agelong processes.

India is used to many religions and regards them as different ways to one goal with a rare tolerance.

Western Christianity is emerging from its isolation and only slowly adjusting its thinking to the fact that not only do other religions exist, but that they persist. Even more, that they are not far away to be the subject of missionary envoys but are close at hand. We have, of course, long had the Jews in our midst, but Europe has often treated them to indifference, at best, and to shameful persecution at worst. Grudgingly it might be admitted that the Jews had a form of religion to which they strangely held fast; their past was sacred history but their present religion could teach nothing. Christianity has faced Islam too, but their relations have not been the happiest. The bloody history of the Crusades offsets Turkish atrocities. When the first crusaders captured Jerusalem in the name of God they massacred nearly all the inhabitants, including women and children, mostly Muslims but even some Jews and Christians. The Muslim world has still not forgotten this evil deed. Misrepresentations of Islam have been very common, even if all did not reach the depths of ignorance shown in the medieval miracle play which depicted Turks worshipping an idol called Baphomet (Muhammad!). Muhammad, whom Muslims regard as the greatest and seal of all prophets, was constantly derided by Christians; even Zwingli who was willing to see Hercules and Socrates in heaven accepted the current slanders about Muhammad, calling him a blind leader of the blind and a slave of sensual pleasures. There have been virtually no attempts to meet Muslims on an equal footing and engage in religious dialogue, with respect to both sides, until quite modern times.

But now not only Judaism and Islam, but all other religions are our neighbours. Hinduism and Buddhism, in particular, demand the attention of Christian theologians and speak in our own streets. Many Europeans and Americans are aware of this, for they have travelled to the East and have seen something of the strength and beauty of oriental faiths in pagoda and mosque, temple and monastery. Some went as missionaries and were impressed despite themselves, others were traders or administrators, and many more went in the armed forces during and after the world wars. They can no longer be put off with stories about heathen darkness, for they often know more than their own clergy about the Asian religions that may receive passing reference in the pulpit on a missionary Sunday. This is not surprising, since most theological colleges for training the clergy give little or no time at all to consideration of any other religion than Christianity. The clergy may know nothing of subjects that interest many laymen, e.g. reincarnation, karma or nirvāna.

But Asian religions are also here in our midst. Not only have many Europeans been to the East, but orientals come to the West in increasing numbers. *The Times* in 1959 printed an article on 'Eastern Faiths in Britain'. This was mostly on London and listed some of the Muslim mosques, Buddhist temples, Rāmakrishna and Shanti Sadan missions, and smaller temples of Sikhs, Parsis, Sūfīs and Bahā'īs. Many of these places of worship exist to serve the spiritual needs of their own followers. But some are openly propagandist and seek to win Europeans from agnosticism or Christianity. In 1959, on the fiftieth anniversary of the English Buddhist Society, was held the first full ordination of Buddhist monks in this country. Previously several English Buddhist monks had been ordained elsewhere. So the East returns the compliment and sends missionaries to the West.

Not only are there these many contacts with other religions, but from the presses a great flow of books and leaflets brings hundreds of thousands of people into touch with oriental religious ideas. Many books have a large sale. A Pelican on *Buddhism*, by Christmas Humphreys, president of the English Buddhist Society, has sold hundreds of thousands of copies. A translation of texts from Buddhist scriptures, not easy reading, in Penguin books, sold out in a few weeks. There are other Penguins on Yoga, Islam and the Koran. Other reputable publishers print popular series of reliable eastern texts. *The Wisdom of the East* series has long provided cheap and good translations of many Asian classics. *The Ethical and Religious Classics of East and West* has similar aims. There is also, it is true, a great deal of cranky and biased 'occult' literature. But anyone who wishes can buy good eastern texts for a few shillings and the new flood of paperbacks brings even more into the market. Some of the earliest and best translations were the work of missionaries, a small minority which had become interested in the faith of the people and their sacred classics. William Carey, Baptist missionary and great linguist, produced one of the first English translations of the great Hindu religious classic the Rāmāyana. Legge translated the Tao Tê Ching, Soothill the Analects of Confucius, Saunders the Buddhist Dhammapada, and so on. But today there are many new translations of these and other scriptures, and there are over fifty of the Bhagavad-gītā in English.

The wide sales of these books testifies to the interest in eastern religions. They show an interest in religion in general, perhaps even a revival of religion, if the Spirit were recognized as blowing where it listeth. Certainly there is a confrontation of religions, and that demands a re-examination of traditional attitudes to other faiths.

'It was in the thirteenth century,' comments E. L. Allen, 'that Western Christendom began to be shaken in the conviction that it possessed the absolute truth. The Church that had converted pagans, excommunicated heretics, and excluded the Jew from the common life, now found herself face to face with Islam.'[1] Islam had existed since the seventh century, however, the Crusades had been fought and had failed, now some attempt was made to understand Islam. However, it came to very little. Francis of Assisi is said to have preached to the Sultan of Egypt, Ramon Lull paid three brief visits to North Africa, and his plans to establish schools of oriental languages in the new universities came to nothing. Nicolas of Cusa, in the fifteenth century, wrote one of the rarest irenical books. In his *De Pace Fidei* he depicts a Christian, a Jew, a Muslim and a Hindu discussing the possibility of a universal religion which will overcome religious differences. But such a synthesis is only a slightly enlarged form of Nicolas's own religion, and like Lull he regards the Qur'ān as simply an imitation of the Gospel. There was no

1 *Christianity among the Religions* (Allen & Unwin, 1960), p. 11.

real dialogue of religions, and certainly not on any wide scale.

The impact of India on the West was only to begin in the early nineteenth century, and then in restricted circles. Most of the early Roman Catholic missionaries to the East lived apart from the people and knew scarcely anything of the religions of the people whom they sought to convert. Outstanding examples, like Roberto de Nobili in India and Matteo Ricci in China who studied the languages and religions of their people and strove to adapt their message to them, were rare indeed and finally either checked by authority or had their work perish with them. Not until 1802 did a Latin translation of the Upanishads, from a Persian version and not from the Sanskrit original, make an impression on Western thinkers and become the solace of Schopenhauer. Indeed this philosopher became so intoxicated with Indian thought that he believed the New Testament must be traceable to an Indian source, and preferred his own bad translation of the Upanishads to better ones that were made from Sanskrit. Protestant missions hardly began till the nineteenth century, there were many misrepresentations of 'heathen blindness', and concentration on abuses. Only in this century has the challenge of Hinduism and Buddhism as systems of religious thought become apparent, and even now it has hardly been taken up at the theological level.

Christianity has faced many conflicts. For the first three centuries there was sporadic persecution of Christians, and the significance of the Cross at the heart of the religion is that it has constantly grappled with suffering and tragedy. In modern times the antagonism with the spirit of the age has left a deep mark, often leading to a divided life wherein the claims of daily life and religion are separated and secularism tolerated. Not only the struggle of science and religion, but the materialist outlook on life and the claims of the state have brought ever-increasing pressure. It is part of the irony of the situation that Christianity has accompanied secularism to other lands, and is sometimes identified with it, a religion of materialism in the eyes of many Asians. But the religious challenge is new, and Christianity tends to regard other religions as rivals without stopping to ask whether they might be allies.

Islam, too, faces trouble in the confrontation of religions and cultures today. A Semitic faith, and almost wholly Asian and African, she has not been isolated to the same degree as Christianity. In India and China she settled alongside other faiths, and in Persia provided a most fascinating example of the fusion of Zoroastrian, Hindu, Christian and Muslim ideas in the Shī'a sects and Sūfī mysticism. Very differently from Christianity Islam was a success religion from its first century. Muhammad and his followers endured persecution until the Hijra, the 'migration' from which Muslim years are counted, brought the support of the community of Medina, the growth of an army, and the subjugation of Mecca and the Arabian tribes within ten years till Muhammad died. The amazing success of the Muslim armies in subduing much of the known world is almost unparalleled. Within a century Mesopotamia, Syria and Persia had fallen, India had been entered, North Africa and Spain overrun and France invaded. These victories were taken as the sign of the presence and power of God and the resultant Arab empire the kingdom of God on earth. Not only was there political and social success, but the new forces created a new culture, incorporating and transforming much of that of classical times. But all this was integrated by religion, Islam was the driving force and religious law regulated all spheres of life.[2]

That was the classic period of Islam which future ages looked back to with pride. It came to an end in 1258 with the fall of Baghdad to the Mongols, but even then Islam converted the conquerors, and after the Arabs new forms were given to Muslim culture by Persians and Turks. The Turkish rule lingered on till the present century when 'the sick man of Europe' collapsed under the pressures of the West and Balkan and Arab nationalism. The Arab countries have succeeded in throwing off the colonizing efforts of the West also, but they find themselves backward, client-states, or subject to 'coca-cola-nisation', suffering under the offensive superiority of British, Americans or Russians. The Muslim

[2] See W. Cantwell Smith, *Islam in Modern History*, pp. 29ff. where this is worked out with great clarity.

peoples, conscious of a great culture and monotheistic religion, find themselves despised as ignorant, dirty or lazy.

There is a profound religious crisis, no less profound for not being easily perceived. Since Islam is the best religion, the latest and crown of them all, and the Arabs have been shown to be the people of God, why are they so low in the modern world, and why do infidel nations flourish? The problem of Western superiority and technical success is a religious problem, for it implies that either the world or Islam must adapt itself. With a tradition of success, rather than suffering, the problem is acute. The most drastic adaptation to modern ways has been made in Turkey, and it involved radical re-shaping or limitation of Islam. Under Kemal Atatürk's revolution the caliphate was abolished, the religious orders dissolved, western legal codes substituted for Islamic sharī'ah, the Latin alphabet adopted, women unveiled, and Turkish replaced Arabic in the call to prayer. There have been uneasy revivals, Arabic has come back, the pilgrimage has increased in numbers, the late prime minister was hailed as a holy man on his escape from an air accident and camels sacrificed for him in the streets of Ankara and Istanbul. But the army coup in 1960 was a challenge to the conservatives and a reaffirmation of the principles of the revolution.

The West tends to be identified with Christianity, just as we tend to call Arabs Muslims. Western missions have made little impact and few converts from Muslim lands. It is tragic that the West generally is blamed for the low state of Arab lands and that few are conscious of Western attempts to understand the East, even in the political sphere, let alone in the religious. Yet the religious challenge is there, and it tends to concentrate on the point at which Muslims are most adamant, the Qur'ān itself. It has been said that the Qur'ān is to Muslims as Christ is to Christianity, the very word of God, and therefore any criticism is inadmissible. But at least translations of the Qur'ān are now permitted, where they were formerly forbidden, as long as they are not used in the mosque. And some small, very small, beginnings have been made at expounding Islam in Western terms and in discussing with members of other faiths some of the common problems of modern times.

India, for over four thousand years, has suffered invasions of armies and religious ideas. About 1500 B.C., before the Hebrew exodus from Egypt, the Aryan invaders with their chariots destroyed the cities of the Indus people, calling them black, snub-nosed and irreligious, and imposing their own Vedic teachings. In time, however, the ancient religion reasserted itself and many features still exist in modern Hinduism. Buddhist, Jain, and other movements arose and were absorbed. The Muslim invasions destroyed thousands of temples and countless images, yet the great Mughal emperor Akbar in the sixteenth century favoured Hinduism more than his ancestral Islam and sought to invent his own eclectic religion, after listening to Jesuit debates on Christianity. British power is recent and comparatively short-lived, the most extensive empire the world has known was also one of the most brief, lasting about a century.

Hinduism today is facing both the secular and the religious challenges that confront other religions. In such a profoundly religious country the scientific, secular outlook of today comes as a challenge to the pre-occupation with the spiritual, and material and social welfare are the concern of many young people. The political and social struggles of this century, leading to independence, have brought women much more into the open and demanded a re-assessment of human relationships. And the sense of nationalism and community has to be joined to a profound desire for progress and world peace. There have been many social reforms, sometimes under the stimulus of Christianity or imposed from above by government, but more deeply led from within by men like Mahatma Gandhi and Vinoba Bhave.

The effect of Christianity has been powerful in education and social reform, less in religion. Christianity has destroyed no temples, as Islam did, and has not spread itself by force. Its greatest successes have been among the outcastes, banned from Hindu temples but welcomed into Christian churches. There has been more dialogue of Christians with caste Hindus than with Muslim or Buddhist leaders elsewhere, but even so it has been small. The reaction of Hinduism in the main has been an attempt to adapt itself to the modern world. Though there is little evidence of significant increase in popular religious zeal, yet small but powerful movements of political and religious reform, like the Hindu Mahāsabhā and the Ārya Samāj, seek to revive Hinduism. Though the Vedānta are the sacred scriptures there has been no short writing which could give a summary like a creed, and efforts are being made to use the Bhagavad Gītā in this way. Teachers (gurus) who in the past remained in their hermitages (āshramas) now come out to instruct seekers after truth and some use modern methods of recording and broadcasting on special occasions. The appearance of another religion, if it is not opposed, is taken as a sign of a different but also valid path to salvation. Thus the edge is taken off the challenge of confrontation. At the same time a new emphasis on 'missionary work', hitherto foreign to Hinduism, appears in the Rāmakrishna and similar missions. These are very conversant with Christian teachings, can quote the New Testament at length, but offer their own way of devotion.

Similarly in Buddhism, there has been the upsetting effect of the contact with the West and Christianity, but trends are less marked than they are in the monotheistic religions. British administrators in Ceylon and Burma, and French in South-east Asia, tended to see in Theravāda (Hīnayāna) Buddhism their own preferences for a rationalistic and unsupernatural religion. They strangely overlooked the fact that the innumerable Buddha images and legends universally held about him were hardly consistent with rationalism and were marks of truly religious worship.

The reaction of Theravāda Buddhism to the new forces was seen in the Buddha Jāyanti (victory) celebrations held from 1954-1956 in Rangoon to mark the 2500th anniversary of the entry of Gotama Buddha into Parinirvāna. Here different versions of the scriptures were collated, arrangements made to translate them into Western languages, and a great World Peace Pagoda built to show that Buddhism had the key to peace.

The fate of Mahāyāna Buddhism has been less happy, except in Japan where it is in close contact with Shinto, new sects, and Christianity. In China and even more in Tibet it has been subject to harsh persecution, and to the attacks of Marxist materialism. With this latter ideology, bringing the latest brand of Western fanaticism, Buddhism has been in sore straits. Its monastic emphasis has not made it easy to fit into a society where productive labour is the rule for all, and in Tibet monasteries have been destroyed and their inhabitants killed, enslaved or deported. Buddhism has undergone similar persecution before in China, particularly under the T'ang dynasty in the ninth century, but it rose again to bring spiritual beliefs to the people.

That other religions besides Christianity are suffering from the close contacts, and secular stresses of today and need adaptation is worth noting. But the fact is perhaps especially difficult for Christians because it is comparatively new for them. Whereas with exploration, trade, imperialism, and missions, all emanating from the West in the past three hundred years, other religions have undergone this process before us, what is called culture-contact or acculturation. But now the confrontation comes back to the West. We live in a multi-cultural context, in which we are one element among others.

This is a hard lesson to learn. For a long time the West has been supreme with other people as inferior. But now with independent states of Asia and Africa, and the great block of China, all emerging, this can no longer be the case. And it applies in religious affairs as in political. 'Christians have tended to think of themselves as secure in a position of authority—with Jews, for instance, as the minor group; or others remote and unobtrusive beyond the seas. In the narrow societies from which most of us come, our English-language group has been supreme. White men have assumed that of course they were dominant; with negroes, for instance, as a minority—to be dealt with in one way or another.'[3]

The resurgence of other nations and other religions brings home another fact: that Christians are in a minority. This is an age of minorities, but it is easier to think of others as the

[3] W. Cantwell Smith, *The Christian and the Religions of Asia*, (International Missionary Council, 1960).

minority than oneself. Christianity is the established religion of England, and it is hard to realize that nevertheless it is a minority religion, since only a small percentage of the population gives it active support. White men have ruled the world, but they were in a minority, and now the coloured races will no longer be dictated to by a small privileged group; like a spoilt child South Africa cries and shuts its eyes rather than face this stern fact. No doubt Communists are in a minority, but the world will not have peace till they recognize this fact. Unbelievers are in a minority, but so are Christians, and Buddhists and Muslims. We have to recognize this to discover with which other minorities we have most in common.

A consequence of the religious minority situation is that there must be at least respect for other faiths. This will be developed in later chapters but one preliminary point may be made here. Cantwell Smith has urged that we drop the phrase 'non-Christian'. It belongs to the days when the world was thought to be divided between ourselves and outsiders, like Anglicans and O.D.'s, or those who like caviar and those who do not. The suggestion of superiority and class privilege which it embodied is completely out-dated, as well as being misleading and essentially false.

A cynic or an atheist may perhaps be described as a non-Christian, but for a devout man of religion the term is out of place. 'It is almost as if one were to introduce the Archbishop of Canterbury by saying "May I present a non-Baptist", or to describe the Roman Catholic Church as non-Presbyterian."[4]

In speaking of religion we are not discussing an abstraction or talking about people who are absent or deaf. We are considering persons, and their faith. 'Fundamentally, I suggest, there are no non-Christians in Asia. There are Muslims, there are Hindus, there are Buddhists.' And their faith can be truly understood not in subservience to our own but as an apprehension of the divine in its own right.

If the religions are now in such close contact, their classics to be found in the bookshops of London and Bombay and every great city, then dialogue between religions, compara-

[4] *ibid.*

tive religion, is forced upon us. The exclusive attitude of the past which regarded its own opinions as supreme and others as not worth discussing is no longer useful, if ever it was. The theological gulf between those who believe, in our way, and those who believe in some other way must be bridged. As we ourselves are in a minority it is no longer valid to divide mankind into 'we' and 'they'. Somehow the gulfs must be closed up and those who care for spiritual things recognize each other's strivings in a community that turns into 'we'.

Once again on the Semitic side, especially in Christianity and Judaism, but not only among Semitic faiths, there have been such exclusive attitudes that dialogue of faiths has been so tardy and difficult. The belief in belonging to a chosen People, and the pride in it, have strongly hindered discussion between religions, and account for the reluctance to take the comparative study of religions seriously. This belief and its concomitants must be looked at now. It is particularly the concern of those of us in the Western tradition. Others may share it in smaller measure. But unless this belief is tackled then this comparative study cannot proceed.

CHAPTER 3

TOLERANCE

If other religions are to be studied it must be fairly and freely. In the past there has been a great deal of prejudice and fanaticism, and the West has only slowly learnt that true liberty demands tolerating people and opinions different from our own.

Arnold Toynbee traces the persecutions that have marred religious and political history in the West back to its Jewish origins. He writes of 'the vein of fanaticism and intolerance which one can see if one looks back on the history of all the Judaic religions: Islam, Christianity and Judaism itself. It is a spirit which does not hesitate to inculcate its doctrine and practice by persecution—a spirit that, in all these three religions, is very shocking to people brought up on Hinduism or Buddhism or some other faith of Hindu origin when they look at the conduct of the western half of the world'.[1] Perhaps he has under-estimated the amount of prejudice and at times persecution that has been known in India and China, and certainly today China and Tibet are subject to most harsh oppression of liberty. It is said that there are no flies in Peking; there is no freedom either. But to see the faults of others does not excuse the blackness of one's own record.

Toynbee is convinced that the Communist totalitarian ideologies are, at least partly, Semitic in origin. 'Communism has taken over from Judaism the myth of the Chosen People; the myth of the miraculous victory of the Chosen People against the heathen who rage furiously together against them; and the myth of the earthly paradise after the victory of Zion has been achieved. These are all Jewish and Christian images of the reality of the spiritual life. They have all been adopted by Communism and have influenced its spirit.'

There is a good deal more to it than that. There is plain lust for power, which Adler has shown, and Bertrand Russell in his study of power, to be a great motive force in human affairs. That power corrupts the best of men, how much

1 *Christianity among the Religions of the World*, pp. 17ff.

more then ordinary mortals, is common knowledge and is plainly visible over half the world today. Religion or ideology may provide its rationale, but the intolerance has numerous causes.

One potent cause is western arrogance, the pride of the Aryan people, of whites over coloured. Cantwell Smith makes 'the indictment that the fundamental defect of our Western, partly Christian society in the view of outsiders is arrogance. The political and economic aspects of imperialism have had more than their share of attention, but are in the end no more important than the human relations between Christendom and the non-Western world, which have been far too much relations of arrogance—sometimes overt and contemptuous, often and still today subtle and unconscious but still disastrous.'[2] The anti-western feeling that is so strong throughout the East is due to this arrogance, and nearer home the treatment of Jews and negroes has the same cause.

This pride of race and colour affected India just as much historically and so is not Semitic but Aryan. The Aryan invaders of India in the sixteenth century B.C. were warriors who oppressed the coloured natives. Their gods were like unto them, fighting, drinking and making love, and never doing a stroke of work. They are akin to the Olympian gods of Greece of whom Gilbert Murray wrote, 'And when they have conquered their kingdoms, what do they do? Do they attend to the government? Do they promote agriculture? Do they practise trades and industries? Not a bit of it. Why should they do any honest work? They find it easier to live on the revenues and blast with thunderbolts the people who do not pay. They are conquering chieftains, royal buccaneers. They fight, and feast, and play, and make music.'[3] So in Vedic times in India the great god Indra fought and drank: 'With all-outstripping chariot-wheel, O Indra, thou far-famed, hast overthrown the twice ten kings of men . . . destroying castle after castle here with strength.' Then like a hard drinking chieftain, 'impetuous as a bull, he chose the *soma*, and in three sacred beakers drank the juices'.

[2] *The Christian and the Religions of Asia*, p. 3.
[3] *Five Stages of Greek Religion* (2nd edn.), p. 67.

The effect of this Aryan invasion was the repression of the natives, socially and religiously. They were called slaves (dāsas), black-complexioned, snub-nosed (anāsa), and indifferent to the (Aryan) gods. The caste-system as it developed was based upon pride of colour, and the very word for caste means colour (*varna*). In religion they were constantly scorned. In the doctrine of reincarnation the Upanishads teach that 'those whose conduct has been evil will quickly attain an evil birth, that of a dog, or a pig, or an outcaste (Chandāla)'. It was forbidden to associate with outcastes, incurring penalties in the next life, and at most food could be placed on the ground for them along with dogs. Marriage outside the caste was forbidden, and always outside the race; the Greeks also held to this, as did the Jews. It is ironical that South Africans now treat Indians and all coloured people in this way, and call them 'kaffirs', an Arabic word that means unbelievers although most black South Africans are Christians.

There is no doubt, however, of the strong Jewish pride of race and religion which eventually affected Christianity. Those rabid nationalists Nehemiah and Ezra forbade racial mingling and tried to dissolve marriages: 'I contended with them, and cursed them, and smote certain of them, and plucked off their hair, and made them swear by God, saying, Ye shall not give your daughters unto their sons.' (Neh. 13, 25). Doubtless they were concerned with the purity of their national religion, but Christianity which sprang from the more liberal wing of Judaism came in time to produce an exclusive spirit and having been persecuted at first then came to persecute others.

There has been an inner conflict, in both Hinduism and the Semitic religions, a conflict of caste-exclusivism and toleration, a conflict of Christian love with the notion of a jealous God. Toynbee says that this has produced a contradiction, reflected in a duality of conduct, which has never been resolved. 'The jealous god's chosen people easily fall into becoming intolerant persecutors. The worshippers of the god who is love—God the merciful, the compassionate—try to act on the belief that their fellow creatures are their brothers, because they are all God's children."[4]

Intolerance is not just something that other people practised, it has left dark stains across centuries of Christian history. The aggressive Crusades, the Inquisition, the massacre of St Bartholomew, the fires of Smithfield, these have left a deep mark and are still not forgotten. It has been said that no other major religious community on earth has shown fiercer intolerance than has the European Christian. The treatment of the Jews has been a constant scandal, culminating in the dreadful holocausts by the Nazis in our own time.

In its relationships with other religions Christianity has often been checked rather than advanced through the harsh methods used by its missionaries. When the Portuguese, the first European explorers of the Asian coasts, went to Ceylon in the sixteenth century they seized hold of the precious relic of the Sacred Tooth of the Buddha. The Buddhists implored them to return it and offered a king's ransom in exchange; but the Portuguese were fanatical in their iconoclasm, they pounded the tooth to pieces, burnt the fragments and scattered the ashes in the sea. The Ceylonese now claim that they got hold of the wrong tooth. But however that may be these ferocious methods, directed by the archbishop of Goa, were not likely to commend the gospel of peace and love.

When the Dutch arrived in Ceylon and ruled it in their turn, they applied persecuting methods with a difference. No child might be educated in school, and nobody hold public office, who had not become a Christian. Hence the feeling that still prevails among the Sinhalese against the mulatto burgher class, which was Christian and held most offices. It is pleasant to know that the British had a better reputation, which time may make clearer, for even mission schools were open to pupils of all faiths and little pressure put on them for conversion. Nevertheless the American theosophist, Colonel Olcott, is honoured by the Sinhalese because he established modern schools for Buddhists. Part of the political struggles of recent times has been to obtain

[4] *op. cit.*, p. 19.

the teaching of Buddhism, the religion of most Sinhalese, in the schools.

In other lands Christian missions have been accused of gaining converts by bribes of material rewards. Such 'rice-Christians', if they have been attracted solely by hope of food, education, and material advancement, are not the best advertisement of the church's methods. On the other hand it is claimed as a Christian duty to feed the hungry, to educate the ignorant, and to welcome outcastes into the churches when they have been forbidden to enter Hindu temples. If all men are equal in the sight of God then there is no place for a caste system in this world. But Mahatma Gandhi fought most effectively for the outcastes, and called them Harijans, 'God's people'.

It must be said, too, that there always have been Christians who have tried to spread their faith in better ways, by understanding and love. Under the same Portuguese a Jesuit missionary, Roberto de Nobili, arrived in India in 1604 to find that the few Christian converts had to renounce all their national customs and culture. The Portuguese 'would not trust the sincerity of their converts unless it was guaranteed by a participation in their meals, loss of caste, change of name and dress, and the adopting of Portuguese customs. Once a man had become a Parangi he was irretrievably compromised in the eyes of his own people; he was looked upon as a traitor, ostracized and cast away; he had no choice but to cling to the Portuguese.'[5] Nobili at once began to adopt Indian ways; he took the dress of a religious ascetic (*sannyāsi*), a vow of poverty which involved renouncing class and life's vanities and riches, his head was shaved and he became a vegetarian. Not only did he learn the Tamil language, but also Sanskrit and the sacred Vedic scriptures. His success was far greater than that of his more ignorant fellow-missionaries, though after his death his methods went into decline until modern times.

In the previous century another Jesuit, Matteo Ricci, had gone to China. He obtained an entry into that forbidden country dressed as a Buddhist priest and later as a Confucian scholar, and became clock-maker to the court of Peking.

[5] V. Cronin, *A Pearl to India* (1959), p. 44.

Ricci sought to extract from the Confucian texts teachings that were compatible with Christianity, and he held that Chinese ancestor cults were not really religious worship or contrary to Christian teaching. But unhappily the rivalries of other catholic orders and Vatican intrigues led in 1704 to papal prohibition of the veneration of Confucius and the ancestors by Chinese Christians. The papal legate, who knew little Chinese, was sent to inform the emperor of China of this decision. 'At the close of the interview the Emperor, a highly intelligent man with a long record of benevolent rule, expressed astonishment that such dunces as Maigrot and Tournon should claim to decide on the meaning of texts and ceremonies of several thousand years' antiquity.'[6] Eleven years later the foreign religion was prohibited in China, and though it lingered on for some years eventually it almost died out till modern times.

In our own day there have been outstanding missionaries who have studied the classics of other religions and sought peaceful intercourse with their followers. A fine example in China was the Lutheran Karl Reichelt, who founded a monastery to which Buddhist monks and followers of any religion could come and meditate among Christian surroundings, without pressure being put upon them. But too many other missionaries have been noted for their foreignness, either their complete lack of interest in the land and its culture, or their scornful condemnation of all its ways. It has been easy to go to outcastes and hill tribes, and act as a benefactor from a superior culture, and have hardly any spiritual dialogue with members of the great scriptural religions, whether in China, Burma, India or Arabia. Undiscriminating contempt for all Asian religions has been only too common.

It is not surprising therefore that Asians commonly accuse Christians of dogmatic intolerance. Christian claims of absoluteness, universal validity, and its call to obedience, meet with strong criticism. This is partly done in a spirit of relativism which regards all faiths as equal, all roads leading to the same goal. Such a spirit would tolerate everything, perhaps cults whose works were plainly evil.

[6] V. Cronin, *The Wise Man from the West*, (1955), p. 282.

But dogmatism itself is condemned and here Christians, particularly fundamentalists and Roman Catholics rise in self-defence. Father Ohm, author of a very frank study in Christian self-criticism, says, 'It is true that Christians, and Catholics in particular, are intolerant where dogmatic theology is concerned; and we consider relativism as mere hedging and a sign of lack of determination. A certain measure of intolerance is characteristic of every genuine dogmatic creed. A religion which abandons the doctrine of absolute truth and uniqueness has surrendered its position and yields to indifferentism. Truth is indivisible and incompatible with error.' This could be understood and justified if he did not then go on to say that the Catholic Church 'rejects the false freedom of conscience inherent in the doctrine of liberal autonomy. . . . We cannot all be allowed to think, to speak and to act as we please according to our limited judgement.'[7] Protestants and Nonconformists know from experience how dangerous such an attitude can prove.

Ohm proceeds to admit that the church has often been intolerant. But he says, 'Even the Church has had to learn her lesson. Today it is Catholic teaching that nobody may be compelled to accept the Faith. The Catholic Church has always condemned that intolerance which means indifference to the truth and the approval of wrong convictions; but in the name of charity, she demands civic tolerance for people holding other faiths and considers respect for every honest conviction a moral duty.' Yet still in Franco's Spain Protestant schools are closed and no portion of the Bible may be circulated; and in Colombia in 1959 it was reported that 116 Protestants had been killed in the last ten years, and over two hundred schools closed or burnt down.[8] Intolerance must be opposed wherever it exists, in Spain or Russia, in South Africa or China. But it hurts more to see it among fellow-Christians.

The Chosen People attitude, that Toynbee sees as productive of so much intolerance, is very widespread. In the religious sphere it is the assumption that God has spoken to

[7] *Asia looks at Western Christianity*, (1959), pp. 37ff.
[8] *Annual Register*, (1959), p. 376.

me and me alone, in the political field that I am right and everyone else is wrong. It is the attitude of the Hyde Park orator caricatured by Baden-Powell, crying 'Down with everybody and up with me.' It contains a large measure of selfishness and pride, that hubris recognized as a fatal flaw in the best of men ever since the Greeks. It has too often effectively undermined the work of Christianity.

But it is by no means confined to the West and, as has been suggested above, it produced the rigidity and exclusivism of the Brahmanical system in India. In India indeed the Chosen People attitude found its fullest expression and was originally based on pride of conquest and colour.

In the Laws of Manu, which have always been recognized as the foremost code of sacred and civil conduct (*dharma*), the privileges and duties of the castes were set out in precise detail, and commandments and avoidances listed with more than levitical scrupulousness. A Brahmin is of the first caste, first-born and lord of creation, an incarnation of the sacred law; whatever exists in the world is the property of the Brahmin and all other mortals exist through his benevolence. The second caste is the warrior and kingly caste (*kshatriya*), the third the farming and trading caste (*vaishya*). These three are the twice-born castes, being born again through initiation with the sacred cord, but of these only the Brahmin may teach the scriptures. The life of the careful Brahmin is hedged about with taboos that must make his life a burden and his mind worried lest he break the law, but these actions ensure him supreme bliss, and he knows that full performance leads beyond the gods to final unity with the divine.

The fourth caste, the Shūdra, has one principal occupation prescribed to it, that of serving the other three meekly. His name must express something contemptible, whereas the Brahmin's is auspicious. If a Brahmin takes a Shūdra wife he will lose his caste and go to hell after death; however, the offspring of such a union, which must often have taken place, rises to the higher caste after the seventh generation. The Shūdra is not initiated nor may he recite the Vedas, though more popular religious texts are open to him. His hope is that by fulfilling his duty he may rise to a higher state in a future incarnation.

But below the Shūdras are the many outcastes, ranked with the animals: a Chandāla, a village pig, a cock and a dog may not look at a Brahmin while he is eating. If a Brahmin touches one such he must purify himself by bathing, muttering sacred verses. Many of the non-caste people follow occupations forbidden to the caste members and have their own dwellings and occupations. But the Chandālas must live outside the village, dressed in the garments of the dead, eating food from broken pots and wandering from place to place. All these depressed classes, or exterior castes, have suffered legal, social and religious disabilities, in some ways like Shūdras but denied the few advantages which would have come to them from belonging to the normal caste system. This is justified by the myth that the caste Hindus were born from the mouth, arms, thighs and feet of the divine person (*purusha*), and all others are their servants.

It can well be understood that with such rigid discrimination social and religious progress was hindered, if not completely barred. Buddhism and Islam in India came to offer equal privileges to all but eventually accommodated themselves to the caste system. The British government preferred not to interfere with native institutions, though missions sought to cut across them and became concerned with outcastes in particular. The modern Indian republic declares that 'the State shall not discriminate against any citizen on the grounds only of religion, caste, sex, place of birth or any of them, and that 'Untouchability is abolished and its practice in any form is forbidden'.

Legislation, however, is not always effective and the caste system remains. Here we are concerned with its religious effects. In Hindu theory the sacred scriptures must not be made known to anyone outside the three twice-born castes; not to Shūdras, women, outcastes, or foreigners. This explains the fact that Hinduism has not been a missionary religion, as Buddhism and Islam have been. But today these scriptures are translated and known to the West, and there are some reforming and missionary sects that seek to spread Hinduism outside India. In its purer forms Hinduism is one of the most attractive of the world's religions, with some of the profoundest insights known to men, but as we have stressed above traditionally it has been rigidly confined to a Chosen People within its own country. If it is to spread it must abandon this Chosen People mentality and all the religious and social discrimination that has accompanied it.

Such pride of religion and revelation has occurred in other religions too, for it is a common human failing. Although Islam recognizes certain other religions, the monotheistic and scriptural faiths, as possessing some divine inspiration and in its best periods has tolerated them, yet it has also sometimes persecuted both Jews and Christians. And towards polytheists or idolaters the traditional Muslim attitude was that of conversion, by force if necessary. The fateful decision of Muhammad to defend the faith by fighting, led to its propagation by the sword. The holy war (*jihād*) gave to Islam its resounding and widespread victories in the early centuries. Unhappily it was also responsible for much destruction and persecution. In north India, for example, so many thousands of Hindu temples were destroyed that many of those that exist now are small and mean, compared with the splendid south Indian temples that survived. How many people were killed as idolaters, or were converted by force cannot be estimated.

Theologians for long, however, in Islam have resisted the attempt to make the holy war an additional pillar of religion. Conditions under which it would be permissible have been laid down meticulously, so that its wanton use is against Islamic law. Today the holy war is interpreted as against sin and its battleground is in the soul. In a fascinating and moving study of the Crucifixion Kamel Hussein depicts the disciples debating whether they should try to save Jesus by force. 'Their determination to give battle and to resist by force increased, to the point where it became difficult for any one of them to counter and oppose it.' Yet Jesus had forbidden them to fight and so others refused to do so: 'I would be opposed to rescuing him if that should involve us in the use of force. For that is the very thing he has forbidden us.'[9] Hussein suggests in a note that this

[9] *City of Wrong*, (Bles, 1960), p. 107f.

dilemma of the disciples and their shame at not rescuing their Master has left a deep mark, a psychological complex, on Christianity ever since. Might one suggest that a related complex is also visible in Islam, of which his own words above are a symptom?

Buddhism has long claimed to be a religion of peace and to be open to all men. Yet such is the temptation to use force to further one's ends that this has been observable to times, though to a much smaller extent than in other religions. The warring monks of Korea entered the political arena with armed bands, and the Japanese reformer Nichiren used most violent expressions about his rivals and urged the government to repress them by force.

Similar observations might be made about other religions. It is one of the tragedies of human nature that when men have been persecuted they often fail to learn the need for tolerance, but given power then proceed to persecute their opponents. Puritans have done this, and so have Jews. Toleration of those of different opinions is one of the hardest virtues to practise. Yet in this world of tyrannical ideologies the necessity for toleration is more clearly visible than ever.

One consequence of the Chosen People attitude has been that the non-elect have been regarded as excluded from grace, till the next life at least in Hinduism, or eternally in some forms of Christianity. But today deeper thinking must be given to this problem, for it goes to the root of religious tolerance.

We have spoken of the confrontation of religions as a new fact of our times. There are serious implications in this. Not only do other faiths exist now and impinge strongly on the West, but it has become clear that they will continue to do so for a long time. Not only the existence but the persistence of these religions must be reckoned with. And with the recognition of this persistence an adjustment of traditional attitudes is necessary.

Christian missions have been at work for nearly two centuries in some eastern countries, but the great masses of the people have remained unchanged in their religious allegiance. In certain Muslim lands missionaries have toiled away for many years to produce a handful of converts, if that. In others groups have been detached to form Christian communities, but the majority has not been affected. The most successful movements have been among outcastes or depressed peoples. It is no accident that Africa has produced the largest Christian harvest and today between twenty and thirty million Africans claim the name of Christian. For the old paganism could not stand up to the strains of modern life and the appeal of a higher culture and literature. The animistic faiths had no literature (because writing was unknown), no long known history, no great temples, and little organization. They were local, based on village and country life, and unsuited to modern towns and industries. So there is a visible 'twilight of the gods', with Christianity and Islam both claiming multitudes in search of a scriptural faith.

But elsewhere, in Islam, Hinduism, and Buddhism, the masses hold to their ancient traditions, and will continue to do so for a very long time yet, at least. 'The evangelization of the world in this generation', once the proud motto of the Student Christian Movement, has not been achieved except in the sense that the Gospel has been preached in many lands. But the harvest has been patchy and in many places almost non-existent.

This means that hundreds of millions of our fellow-creatures are not and will not be Christians. What will be their lot? This is a blunt question, but inherent in missionary work and it must be faced.

There are still those who are willing to accept the damnation of the majority of mankind with apparent equanimity. Fundamentalist missions generally hold to this. And it goes with the assumption that other religions are the work of the Devil, and that studying them is playing with fire, hell-fire. The Cables and others in China explicitly held this notion, and it is one more example of western arrogance that so repels many Asians and makes them think that Christian charity is a mockery.

The Athanasian creed was long recited as stating that unless everyone keeps the Catholic Faith 'whole and undefiled, without doubt he shall perish everlastingly'. However, this creed has fallen from favour, and the 1928 translation brought significant changes that made it a more personal confession, 'a man' instead of 'every one', and 'everlastingly' was changed to 'eternally', which could mean the duration of an age.

The Roman Catholic church has held formally to the old position. All unbelievers, and that would include Protestants, must go to Hell. The noblest of pagans, because he is unbaptized, could not rise out of Hell to Purgatory. Dante showed this by putting Virgil and Socrates in Hell, and even the Muslim Saladin, but in the highest circle where they suffered little pain except deprivation of heaven: 'they sinned not, and though they have merit it suffices not, for they had not baptism which is the portal of the faith.' However many Roman Catholics today speak of the 'baptism of desire' which good men may be supposed to have and whose lives seem to fit them for more than Hell.

Most modern Christians would be reluctant, if pressed, to accept that most of mankind is doomed to everlasting torment and would regard such a harsh doctrine as the product of an unenlightened and intolerant age. Supposing that some twenty or thirty per cent of mankind are Christians, what of the other seventy per cent? Are they to be damned? What should we think of a state in which seventy per cent of the population was in prison? Should we not think that something was wrong with the government? Then is not something wrong with the government of the universe if most men are destined to perdition?

The conclusion of large-scale damnation is the result of a perverted and narrow notion of salvation. No doubt Christian practice often falls short of ideals, but here something is wrong with the ideal itself, if it is orthodox. 'Running through almost all of this,' says Cantwell Smith, 'is the distorted ideal itself—the basic doctrine that we are saved, outsiders are damned . . . The problem is serious. So far, no theological answer to it has been given. The doctrine of the Church has traditionally appeared to be that non-Christians are going to Hell. Not many modern Christians really believe this any more, but no clear alternative has been formulated by the Church. And adequate alternatives have hardly been seriously put forward by representative thinkers. In other words, the Christian community is at the moment theologically unequipped for living in the twentieth century, with its pluralist mankind.'[10]

Other religions have to face the same problem. Brahmins, and Muslims in particular. But Christians, who will form the majority of the readers of this book, and missionary societies and their advocates, must make up their minds, and adjust their thinking. It may well be asked whether the Hell-fire picture really is consistent with the Gospel of love, but these theological issues must be worked out carefully.

Our concern here is to stress the urgency of new and constructive theological thinking, in the light of the confrontation of religions today. And we would also stress the importance of tolerance, in theology as in action, and urge Christians, Muslims, Hindus and Buddhists to respect each other's beliefs, without waiting for the theologians.

[10] *The Christian and the Religions of Asia*, p. 3f.

CHAPTER 4

THE ATTITUDE TO OTHER RELIGIONS

The necessity for determining the proper attitude to be adopted towards the persistent and resurgent Asian religions, is observable in the number of books which have approached the subject from varying points of view. In 1938 Hendrik Kraemer of Leiden published for the International Missionary Council his trenchant *Christian Message in a Non-Christian World.* This was followed in 1953 (Hulsean Lectures 1949) by E. C. Dewick's *Christian Attitude to other Religions,* much more conciliatory than Kraemer. In 1958 came both A. C. Bouquet's *Christian Faith and Non-Christian Religions,* and Arnold Toynbee's *Christianity among the Religions of the World,* and in 1960 E. L. Allen's *Christianity among the Religions.*[1] And now Cantwell Smith, Huston Smith, K. W. Morgan, Philip Ashby, and others in America continue to give their minds to this urgent problem.

Part of the divergence of opinion among the above writers is a reflection of a division within Christianity itself. This stems from the Calvinist revival and the teaching of Karl Barth in particular, and links up with the older fundamentalist missionary attitude. The uncompromising character of the Barthian school was perhaps natural in its historical setting, for the 'German Christians' under Hitler were coming to an accommodation with the state and appealing to reason rather than revelation to justify their position. Barth maintained that the Christian revelation was not to be questioned, for that is sinful pride and the revealed Word of God must be accepted. If it were asked how the Word of God could be recognized, the answer would be that one cannot judge, for man is utterly corrupt. This seems to lead straight to determinism and rigid Calvinism: God chooses some and damns others. Most Christians, and in Protes-

[1] See Neill's fine *Christian Faith and Other Faiths* (1961)

tantism the Arminian and Anglo-Saxon thinkers, do not accept such extreme doctrines.

In face of other religions and their claim to serve God in different ways, Barth will not admit the genuineness of the claim. Religion, as distinct from Christianity, 'is unbelief; it is the work of godless man.' Even Muslims, who are monotheists and share part of our Jewish inheritance, are rejected: 'the God of Muhammad is an idol like other idols.' We seem to be back in the Middle Ages. And so Barth will not allow any 'points of contact' between Christianity and any other religion, only a complete breach is possible.

Some modification of the Barthian teaching may be seen in the writings of Emil Brunner on natural theology, and particularly in his *Revelation and Reason* (Zurich 1941). Brunner does not reject, as Barth does, the possibility of some form of general revelation, or perhaps intuition, outside Christianity. But he contrasts it keenly with the vertical special revelation given by 'the God of the Bible, the God who seeks man'. Even Islam is rejected as containing special revelation, apart from what it has derived from the Bible through Judaism and Christianity. Only in Christianity is there a revelation that claims to have universal validity, and only once has God revealed himself completely. The failure to take Islam seriously is the weakest spot in this argument. The insistence on the uniqueness of the Bible can be met by even stronger counter-claims on behalf of the Qur'ān, and the result would be opposing dogmatisms that cannot speak to one another. Even the slight concessions allowed by Brunner to the apprehensions of reason, however, were denied by Barth with an angry, No. This was the voice of the serpent, he declared; there is no knowledge of God from reason, and the attempt to find it is meaningless and sinful.

These dogmatic arguments disturbed the theological world considerably, and those concerned with missionary work in Asia sought for guidance in their contacts with other religions. So Hendrik Kraemer was commissioned to prepare a volume for the guidance of the World Missionary Conference, held at Tambaram in India in 1938. One of the most surprising features in this book is the brief foreword by William Temple, then Archbishop of York, in which he said that 'It will bring new confidence to many who are perplexed, and supply the principles of missionary policy for our generation'. Since Temple's own position was quite different, and Kraemer later criticized Temple's own Gifford lectures on general and special revelation, one wonders, as Bouquet suggests, whether Temple had given careful scrutiny to what he commended.

Kraemer agrees with Barth that there are no 'points of contact' between Christianity and other religions. Although he makes slight reservations on full Barthianism, he is just as convinced that there is no real revelation of God outside the Bible. All the non-biblical religions, if not sin, are what he calls 'naturalist religions of trans-empirical realization'. This cryptic phrase is meant to indicate that men in these religions try to save themselves, to become divine, and have no authentic revelation from God. Kraemer had worked as a missionary in Indonesia, but his experience of Islam there had not convinced him of the reality of its claims. His attitude would lead, as we have noted on Brunner above, to a head-on collision of these two faiths which both believe in the revelation of the transcendent God in a sacred book—only different books. The claim of Islam is just as sweeping as that of any Calvinist, and its doctrine of predestination brings it strangely parallel to that Christian heresy. What can be said by such opposing faiths? The well-known story of the Presbyterian elder arguing with the Jesuit suggests the only answer: 'We must agree to differ. We are both trying to serve God; you in your way, and I in his.'

It must be said of the Muslim that if his religion will have no truck with idolaters yet it has always traditionally honoured other 'religions of a book'; Jewish, Christian, and Zoroastrian. Would that the Barthian were at least as charitable. And if a religion is known by its fruits, and the greatest of these is charity, then there must be something wrong with a religion that condemns all other faiths, and with them the greater part of mankind, to hell.

Much more charity is shown by the Jewish mystic Martin Buber who writes, 'all God's names are hallowed'. And there is the other wing of Christian thought, indeed a broad stream of Christian belief and action down the ages, that recognizes the light of God 'at sundry times and in divers manners'.

Kraemer's book caused an immediate division in the missionary council, and while some welcomed his views others strongly opposed them. In the main the Calvinists and Lutherans from the Continent supported the Barthian viewpoint, and the Anglo-Saxons opposed it. But more significant was the opposition of many Asian delegates, Indian, Chinese and others who strongly dissented from the Barthian condemnation of the traditional religions and cultures of their countries. A good deal was written then and later about the need for a more sympathetic attitude.

At an earlier missionary conference, in Jerusalem in 1928, there had even been delegates who urged the co-operation of Christians and members of other religions in face of the rising secularism of today. Then in 1932 had come a report entitled *Re-thinking Missions*. This was the product of a concern among American Protestants about the future work of missions, and their relationship to the religions of Asia. The most important member of this commission was W. E. Hocking, and here and in his later *Living Religions and a World Faith* he looks towards a single world religion, in agreement with the trend towards a world government. If this does not mean a synthesis of faiths, at least it demands 'reconception' on the part of leaders of all faiths and accepting help from others to distinguish what is vital and what is secondary in our own faith.

Kraemer's book, and his later *Religion and the Christian Faith* (1956), must be seen also then as reactions against what he regards as extreme liberalism.[2] This is noticeable also in his treatment of the Bible. For although Kraemer pretends not to be a fundamentalist, and declares himself willing to accept the results of biblical criticism, in fact his emphasis on 'biblical realism' leads him close to a doctrine of verbal inspiration, as for example in his acceptance of the early chapters of Genesis without reference to authorship and date. His individualistic treatment and neglect of church teaching lead him to extremes and lay him open to

[2] See also his *World Cultures and World Religions* (1960)

considerable criticism. So his critics say that he argues in circles and evades the real problems of the confrontation of religions.[3]

Kraemer's reaction is only typical of one wing of Christian thought, and he himself admitted that even at the Tambaram Conference his views had made 'appallingly small' progress. Canon Dewick was a missionary in India and in his *Christian Attitude to Other Religions* he seeks to face the challenge of other faiths and suggests certain reforms of missionary policy. Some of his most interesting discussions are on verses from the Bible which have seemed to suggest complete exclusiveness for the Christian claim, such as, for example, 'neither is there any other name under heaven, given among men, whereby we must be saved'. (Acts 4, 12). He disposes of the mere use of the verbal form of the name 'Jesus', which differs from language to language. He quotes the Quaker Robert Barclay, who argued against the Calvinists that even heathens might be saved. Confronted with this text Barclay replied: 'Though they knew it [the name of Jesus] not outwardly, yet if they knew it inwardly, by feeling the virtues and power of it, they are saved by it . . . Salvation lieth not in the literal, but the experimental knowledge.' But more significant is Dewick's suggestion that the Word of God, Christ, is to be found far beyond the New Testament, operative in creation, in the Old Testament, and beyond.

This Logos-doctrine, applied to other religions, is supported in a remarkable way in the writings of Archbishop Temple. In one of his last books he wrote, 'By the word of God—that is to say by Jesus Christ—Isaiah and Plato, Zoroaster, Buddha, and Confucius, uttered and wrote such truths as they declared. There is only one Divine Light, and every man in his own measure is enlightened by it.'[4]

Isaiah was not a Christian, in the sense that he lived in the pre-Christian Jewish dispensation, yet he has long been regarded as a forerunner of Christ and his words are treasured in the Christian Bible. Plato is the father of western philosophy and has long since been baptized into

[3] See P. Chenchiah, *Re-thinking Christianity in India* (Madras, 1938).
[4] *Readings in St. John's Gospel*, i, p. 10.

Christianity, so to speak. Zoroaster was a monotheist, and as such especially acceptable to Christian scholars who have regarded him as akin to the biblical prophets or Muhammad. Buddha and Confucius were very different, and their teachings are strange to the Semitic point of view. Yet they both believed profoundly in the spiritual order of things, and their truths must come from God, if all truth comes from the one Divine Light.

Before Temple the Swedish Archbishop Söderblom had given a great deal of thought to the problem of the truths of other religions, which he summed up in his Gifford Lectures in the year he died, 1931, *The Living God*. Söderblom is concerned to inquire not only if God reveals himself to other peoples, but does he continue to reveal himself. He regards as absurd the notion that divine revelation was finished in the Bible. God is the living God, and as man is always seeking him, so he is always responding to men. Indeed any other view would be a denial of the nature and activity of God, as love and living. Creative genius in man is a mark of the continued creativity of God. The Logos-doctrine, which had been taught in the early Church by such men as Justin Martyr and Origen, had been eclipsed, but now is the time for its re-emergence, and now theology must discover it again in the light of the modern knowledge of other faiths. All mankind shares in the inspiration of the Logos, or Christ, all religions are rooted in the self-disclosure of God and all genuine religious experience comes from God. Indeed he says that if there is no revelation outside the Bible, then there is none within the Bible. Temple later said the same, 'unless all existence is a medium of revelation no particular revelation is possible . . . Only if God is revealed in the history of Syrians and Philistines can he be revealed in the history of Israel.'

With these two great archbishops championing the Logos-doctrine and the universal revelation of God it is not surprising that many Christians cannot accept the Barthian and fundamentalist condemnation of all other religions. The debate continues, and in his *Christian Faith and Non-Christian Religions* A. C. Bouquet has summarized many of the arguments to date by writers on different sides. But he closed his study some ten years ago and a great deal more is now being written.

From the Roman Catholic standpoint R. C. Zaehner sees other religions besides Judaism as preparations for the Gospel. Both Zoroaster and Muhammad were true prophets, and there is no attempt to disparage the latter as was so often done in the past, but to understand his religious experience and teaching. 'However much you may misunderstand or disapprove of the Qur'ān, you cannot ignore it. Not even in the Old Testament do you have such an overmastering insight into Omnipotence. . . . That Muhammad was a genuine prophet and that the authentic voice of prophecy made itself heard through him, I for one find it impossible to disbelieve on any rational grounds—assuming, of course, that God exists and makes Himself known through prophets.'[5]

Zaehner notes that Christians have found Muhammad a stumbling-block and have preferred to by-pass him, yet Muhammad's Semitic religion is nearer to us than that of India and beyond. But Zaehner sees God revealed 'at sundry times and in divers manners', giving the words of the Epistle to the Hebrews a much wider extension than that of reference to Old Testament prophets. He claims that there is a 'Gospel according to the Gentiles', and partial revelations of God which fall into place when seen perfected in Christ.

Beyond the Semitic religions those of India are the most impressive, indeed the Indian tradition is the other main stream of human religious thought, after that of Israel. It is strange that Christianity has recognized the virtues of Greek philosophy, indeed has taken it into its own philosophical system, but has been slow and wary in welcoming the much more profoundly religious insights of the Indian religions. 'It would, however, be more natural for us, who during the last two centuries have become aware of the sacred literature of the Asiatic peoples, to look for the *praeparatio evangelica* not so much among the Greeks as among the nations of Asia; for it is Asia that is the birthplace of every single religion that has withstood the test of time.' So he claims that 'of the revelations outside Israel the most im-

[5] *At Sundry Times* (1958), p. 27.

pressive is undoubtedly the progressive revelation in India which showed to man first that there is one principle which informs both the cosmos and the human soul, secondly that the human soul is immortal, and finally that there is a personal God.'[6]

Zaehner regards the religions of Asia as preparatory to Christianity where 'the highest insights of both the Hindus and the Buddhists are fulfilled.' But to regard other religious truths as subservient to one's own smacks of patronage. It is to take too narrow a view of religion, as if all that mattered was one's own viewpoint. That multitudes have found help and inspiration in other religious traditions must be taken into account.

E. L. Allen, in *Christianity among the Religions*, speaking partly as a philosopher-theologian and partly from his experience as once a missionary in China, is anxious that full value should be accorded to the spiritual structures of Hinduism, Buddhism and Islam, and that they should not be dismissed except as they relate to Christianity. 'The great religions are to be accepted for their own sake and not for the tribute they pay to our religion. What they say to us is not decisive for their worth but what they have said to the multitudes who found shelter and inspiration in them.' There are other lines of development besides our own which have their own value. And as with the religious systems, so with their founders and teachers, 'Confucius and Buddha claim attention in their own right and not merely for the service they can render to Christianity.'[7]

Such an attitude is of great importance today, when the religions impinge upon each other as never before. New lines of truth appear, which may strengthen or challenge our own faith. But to understand them they must be studied in their own context and in the light of the worship of their devotees. The Gītā, the Dhammapada or the Qur'ān are not mere historical curiosities, or texts for language study, or objects of missionary attack. They are the centre of the devotion of countless millions, whose lives even now are strengthened by their teaching.

[6] *ibid.*, pp. 165f., 183.
[7] pp. 124, 126.

These theological attitudes, and the missionary policies that spring from them, are not merely of ecclesiastical interest as showing that one belongs to one party or another. They affect the study of comparative religion. For not only are there those who are actively engaged in the confrontation of religions involved, as priests or missionaries, but how they think and act affects others whose interest may be more academic. If intolerance is to hold the field then serious study will be affected. But a more sympathetic attitude can be of help to both sides, and we have noted how some of the early missionaries interested themselves in the religious classics of their people and made careful and fair translations of them.

Toynbee, who approaches the subject as a historian, yet who feels the great importance of inter-religious dialogue, has insisted upon the necessity of charity and abandonment of intolerance. He quotes with approval the plea of Symmachus, the Roman orator and defender of the old faith, in his argument for tolerance against the suppression of his religion by the secular arm of the Christian Roman government. Pleading with Ambrose, Symmachus said that the greatness of the divine necessitated different approaches to truth: 'The heart of so great a mystery cannot ever be reached by following one road only.' Although Symmachus lost his cause and the ancient paganism was suppressed, on the surface at least, yet his plea reappears in face of the many religions of today. Toynbee says that 'he has not even been silenced; for although Symmachus' ancestral religion is long since extinct, Hinduism lives to speak for Symmachus today.' And he concludes his long study of the historian's approach to religion by claiming, from the standpoint of a Western historian, 'We can take Symmachus's words to heart without being disloyal to Christianity. We cannot harden our hearts against Symmachus without hardening them against Christ. For what Symmachus is preaching is Christian charity.'[8]

[8] *An Historian's Approach to Religion*, pp. 295-7.

CHAPTER 5

TRUTH AND ERROR

Whether a religion is true or false could, at best, only be decided after full study of all its doctrines and practices, and not by dogmatic assertion without examination. By this standard many theologians have failed in their duty to examine the evidence about other religions before asserting that Christianity alone is true and that all other religions are false.

'There is not anyone alive,' says Toynbee, 'who is effectively in a position to judge between his own religion and his neighbour's.' This is from the man who has made the greatest modern studies of world movements and historical processes. He proceeds to substantiate his statement by considering the many subtle influences of heredity and environment that must sway a man to give more favourable consideration to the religion in which he was brought up, and which make complete impartiality almost impossible. 'An effective judgement is impossible when one is comparing a religion which has been familiar to one in one's home since one's childhood with a religion which one has learnt to know from outside in later years. One's ancestral religion is bound to have so much the stronger hold upon one's feelings that one's judgement between this and any other religion cannot be objective.'[1]

This view may be surprising, and even shocking, in the light of traditional theology and much missionary propaganda, yet a little reflection should show that it is reasonable. And for scholarly study it is essential to avoid any judgement that has a suspicion of prejudice. So the impulse to pass judgement must be restrained, at least until we know another religion so well that we can view it from within.

The historian sees Christianity as historically conditioned and therefore relative, whereas orthodoxy has tended to lift Christianity out of history and set it apart from all other religions as a supernatural irruption into history, testified to

1 *ibid*, p. 296.

by miracle and prophecy. The appeal to miracle is not so prominent today, and certainly much less so when considering missionary progress. The victory of Christianity in Europe used to be attributed largely to its superior proficiency in miracle-working, such as when St Patrick destroyed all the snakes in Ireland. But others can play at this game. 'We, too, have such miracles', they will say, 'We even have greater ones. Buddha worked and lived such miracles as would make all Christian miracles look very insignificant indeed.'[2]

The historical conditioning of a religion means that there is no such thing as 'pure' Christianity; all forms of it have been changed through the centuries of development. The German theologian Troeltsch maintained that this historical conditioning invalidates all attempts at judging other religions. For our claim that Christianity is higher than other religions is no more than an assertion that our civilization is higher. And even then this claim is not objective. We find and praise in a religion and culture just what we want to find. An Indian would be able just as well to claim the superiority of Hinduism, as many do, because he would look for the marks of civilization that appear to him superior; non-injury and tolerance as better than technical ability. It would not even help to ask an atheist for an 'impartial' opinion, for if he were a European he would be a 'Christian atheist', swayed by the traditions of western culture. Nietzsche is a case in point. So of the religions Troeltsch concluded, 'the question of their several relative values will never be capable of objective determination, since every proof thereof will presuppose the special characteristics of the civilization in which it arises.'[3]

The theologian E. L. Allen finds this argument 'unanswerable'. If one takes a Christian standard then of course other religions will fare less well than Christianity. It is like an examination in which one does better than its rivals, because it has set all the questions, and is both counsel and judge in its own case. But other religions can use the same

[2] Ohm, *Asia looks at Western Christianity*, p. 1.
[3] *Christian Thought*, p. 33.

methods, and the result is a return to opposing dogmatisms that refuse to listen to each other.

Other theologians would not agree with Allen, and certainly the general opinion in the past has been that Christianity is true, and alone is true. There are dangerous implications here, which are likely to be severely criticized today and to have a boomerang effect upon theology. It was all very well in the past, when very little was known of any other religion, and much of that was so distorted that, for example, Muslims could be represented as worshipping an idol called Mahomet! But today so many people have first-hand knowledge of Asian countries, and so much cheap and accurate literature is available about Asian religions, with their classics translated and well known, that ignorance can no longer be accepted as an excuse for shabby treatment of beliefs that men hold dear.

That Christianity is true is a necessary article of Christian faith and a defensible proposition. That it has the only truth means that other religions are in error, perhaps completely so. This indeed is the Barthian position; other religions are 'sin', the 'work of godless man', humanistic attempts at raising man to the divine level.

The implications of the extreme position are that there is no good at all in either the teaching or the practice of other religions. There is no natural theology, or any other form of revelation. The Gentiles cannot, as St Paul would have them, 'show the work of the law written in their hearts, their conscience bearing witness therewith.' (Rom. 2, 15).

But if common observation, as distinct from dogmatic assertion, sees men of other faiths living good lives, in the light of dogmas some of which appear not unreasonable nor unspiritual, then either the Barthian must deny all these good works or else admit his argument wrong and perhaps his own salvation imperilled. So, says Cantwell Smith, 'when an observer comes back from Asia, or from a study of Asian religious traditions, and reports that, contrary to accepted theory, some Hindus and Buddhists and some Muslims lead a pious and moral life and seem very near to God by any possible standard, so that so far as one can see in these particular cases at least faith is as "adequate" as

Christian faith, then presumably a Christian should be overjoyed, enthusiastically hopeful that this be true."[4]

The tragedy is that the Barthian cannot be overjoyed, for if he admits some truth or goodness to others then his own faith is in danger. 'One becomes walled up within the quite intolerable position, that the Christian has a vested interest in other men's damnation.' The effect of such theology upon the belief in a God of love is deadly. The 'terrible decree' of Calvinism, against which Wesley so often wrote, ends by destroying the central belief of Christianity, which is that God is love, to all men and at all times.

Rather than rejoicing in the manifest signs of the presence and revelation of God 'at sundry times and in divers manners', in a 'Gospel according to the Gentiles', one finds people afraid lest it be found that other nations and religions produce spiritual men. There is an emotional resistance to the news of moral lives among men of other religions, yet also a fear that it might be true. If they will not declare, like the Cables and Pattersons, that all religions are of the devil and study of them dabbling in evil, yet many people prefer to stop their ears and ignore the facts.

One would have thought that news of holy and moral men in other lands would be cause for rejoicing, that reform of religion would be welcomed, and revival of religion taken as a sign that in the battle with materialism there are valuable allies on our side. This point will be considered further in a later chapter. For the moment let us consider the charity explicit in St Peter's declaration: 'Of a truth I perceive that God is no respecter of persons: but in every nation he that feareth him and worketh righteousness is acceptable to him.' (Acts 10, 34-5).

Perhaps the contrary attitude to the Barthian may come to hold the field; that signs of the action of God in other religion will be welcomed. Indeed, this would seem to be inherent in the belief in a God of love, for such a God cannot have left himself without witness. And it should hardly be possible to hold a full Christian faith without believing that God has spoken to other men than those of one's own race and religion, in different times and ways. If this is not

[4] *The Christian and the Religions of Asia*, p. 6.

true, then Christian teaching itself is false. The Jews vehemently denied the claims of the Samaritans to serve God in their own temple and by their own traditions. But in his parable Jesus showed a Samaritan who had more charity than the orthodox priest or levite, and better knowledge of the commandment to love one's neighbour.

So, with Cantwell Smith, we would 'plead that we abandon, as utterly unworthy, the traditional notion that if Christianity is true, then it must follow that other faiths are false—or at the least inadequate.' This need not mean that one's own faith is to be held the less firmly, or that all religions are of equal value, or equally good ways to the truth. 'The lamps are different, but the light is the same,' said the Sūfī Rūmī. Some of the lamps may be small, and others darkened with age and in need of cleaning. But there is one true Light, 'which lighteth every man'.

Far too long have religions, especially in the West, been passing judgement upon others. They have claimed superiority for themselves, judges in their own cause, and have not had the humility to recognize that claims of superiority and inferiority are not admissible. The religious man must not measure himself against others, even those of other religions, and thank God that he is not 'as this publican'. He must look only to the divine holiness and realize how inferior he himself is to that.

Toynbee claims also that Christianity should be purged of the traditional view that it is unique. 'We have to do this if we are to purge Christianity of the exclusive-mindedness and intolerance that follows from a belief in Christianity's uniqueness.'[5] He sees this as not merely a western accretion or deformation of Christianity but a congenital feature, inherited from Judaism and also partly shared by Islam. The notion of God as a jealous God, the God of my tribe, or my church, has led on to an exclusiveness that bans God from all other faiths, and sects, than my own. This exclusive-mindedness is one of the main causes of persecutions, crusades, inquisitions, and the rest which have given church history so many sorry pages.

[5] *Christianity among the Religions of the World*, p. 96f.

One has heard the history of the Church described as the greatest argument against Christianity, yet proving its truth because the religion has persisted despite all the weaknesses of its followers. And there is the story of the Jew who visited medieval Rome and was converted to catholicism; such an institution must be divine, he said, for otherwise such corruption could not endure.

This is poor casuistry and unlikely to appeal to modern men, who are prone to judge Christianity by its own standards, and condemn the Church by the Sermon on the Mount. Unless Christianity produces works that are in some way commensurate with its teachings then it also is likely to be rejected as false.

Toynbee's use of the word 'unique' needs some examination. Apparently he means it to indicate the view that Christians have 'the sole and unique revelation', and he pleads for a recognition that there are other revelations. 'If God loves mankind, He would have made a revelation to us among other people. But, on the same ground and in virtue of the same vision of what God's nature is, it would also seem unlikely that He would not have made other revelations to other people as well.'[6] It is possible to be convinced of the truth of one's own religion, and the rightness of its demands, and receive these as revelations from God, and yet at the same time to recognize that these are not unique. In other words religion can be held as true, and yet without the implication that other faiths are beyond the pale and only fit for extirpation.

But to be 'unique' may mean more than this. Certain of its doctrines Christianity shares with other faiths: belief in God, in forgiveness of sins, in eternal life. These are common within the Semitic tradition, and to some degree beyond it.

But Christians would claim that there is at least one unique element in Christianity, and that is Christ himself. He is the Special Revelation of God that some theologians have distinguished from General Revelations made to other peoples.

There is some difference in such an attitude between that of Christianity and of other religions, though perhaps even

[6] *ibid.*

then not so much as might be supposed. The Muslim accepts many prophets of God, including Moses and Jesus the Christ; but he regards Muhammad as the greatest of all prophets, completing and surpassing them, and second only to God. The Hindu believes in many avatars of the divine, including the Buddha, but generally the Hindu regards Rāma or Krishna as the greatest of all. The Buddhist believes in many Buddhas, not in the one Gautama of 'history', and in at least one Buddha to come—Maitreya; but Gautama is the greatest for this age.

Thus there is a recognition of other revelations or teachers, but also a claim to uniqueness for the leaders of the particular religions. The same applies to the scriptures, especially to the Qur'ān, which is revered more by Muslims than the Bible is by Christians. But a parallel claim to uniqueness would be made by Hindus for the divinely-inspired Vedas, and for the Tripitika or Lotus Sūtra by the Buddhists.

If these distinctive elements, which differentiate the religions from one another, were removed, they would lose their distinctive note. So that what is needed is the tolerance that recognizes the validity of claims to have other revelations than our own, partly as preparatory, but also in their own right as aspects of truth. But the truly unique and singular elements in the religions will be upheld by their followers.

The important thing is to get beyond attacking and denigrating other faiths. Muhammad has been a target for such unkind and misunderstanding Christian comment in the past, that it is time there was a change. Zaehner's open welcome for Muhammad as a true prophet is a big step in the right direction. The attitude adopted by Christians towards other churches, at its best, may be helpful in relations between religions. When J. H. Newman, still an Anglican priest, began to see something of the truth of the Roman church, he resolved never to speak or write against it. It is not necessary to relax one's own faith a whit to adopt such a self-denying ordinance in relationships between religions. In times of peace policy alone demands that diplomats be polite with former enemy states. Cannot the same apply even more between seekers after spiritual truth?

Further, there is the danger that in claiming one religion as absolute, and thereby banning others, one may be undermined by the divisions within the religion itself. If one religion is absolute, or the highest development, to which form of the religion does one refer? The Roman Catholic will have no doubt of his own superiority, but the Orthodox and the Protestant would disagree. The philosopher Hegel tried to demonstrate that the history of religion culminated by logical development in Christianity as the absolute religion. But within Christianity he believed his own peculiar interpretation of Lutheranism to be the supreme form, and an Anglican would smile at that.

When we make a claim for the supremacy of Christianity that means Christianity as we understand it, and in the long run that gives too great importance to our own opinions. H. R. Mackintosh, however, believed that one could speak of an 'empirical Christianity' which is quite apart from personal opinion and tradition and that this is absolute. This stands 'not for the reaction of man but for the action of God', as expressed in certain cardinal doctrines.[7] But these doctrines, all of which have been disputed at different periods of the history of the Church, are human expressions of ineffable things. What is described here is not 'the action of God' but the 'reaction of man' to it, and the sets of doctrines that have been evolved have found many interpretations, many variations of them being still found today in the different churches.

Religions contain unique elements, but these are mediated in such fallible ways that the religion cannot be described as absolute. It is often insisted that Christianity is historical, it was Jewish in the first century, and expanded into the Greek and pagan world, and finally became predominantly European. It had to adapt itself in the past, and has to adapt itself today if it is to commend itself to men of different lands and cultures. It has to pay what Hocking calls 'the price of existence'. Mahāyāna Buddhism was similarly transformed in Tibet and Japan, and Islam in Persia and Africa. So concludes, Allen, 'Nothing in this world of space and

[7] *Types of Modern Theology*, p. 215f.

time is absolute. Only God himself is. An absolute religion is a contradiction in terms.'[8]

If this is so then one must be all the more gentle when considering other religions, and beware of being swayed by prejudice which comes from one's own cultural background and ingrained habits of thought. The ideal given in the Gospels, 'judge not that ye be not judged', should not only apply between individuals but between religions as well.

Does this mean that there is then to be no comparison between religions? Are we to be simply spectators of a free-for-all in which each dogmatism conducts a lonely battle in support of its own uniqueness? Kraemer would not allow our reason or our moral sense the right to form any judgements at all upon the signs of divine revelation. And certainly it must be allowed that reason has its limits, but this is very different from refusing to use it or to recognize its validity, and Kraemer himself reasons carefully and so appeals to reason.

If we have now attained a spirit of humility, and a suspicion of prejudice, by agreeing that religions have a right to their own peculiar dogmas, then the way is cleared for more fruitful discussions than in the past. Clearing away fanaticism and contradictions should allow for a much more free communication between religions. And this communication is between persons, not just between abstract systems.

In the past when one spoke of comparative religion, or the study of religions, it might be assumed that the audience was wholly Western. That can no longer be taken for granted, but almost the opposite holds. The audience is worldwide and contains many members of the religions to which reference is made. There can be no more cheap gibes, or funny cracks at exotic features of other faiths. The utmost care must be taken with every reference and comparison. In an article on Religious Instinct R. C. Zaehner compared Muhammad with Hitler, and was indignantly taken to task by the Imām of the Woking Mosque as bringing unnecessary bitterness into Muslim-Christian relation-

[8] *op. cit.*, p. 128.

ships. When speaking of a 'religion', one is not referring to a historical curiosity, but to a faith by which men live and beings in whom they put their trust.

Comparative religion is more necessary than ever, it is essential. But more than ever it must be conducted in a spirit of grace and charity. In those universities that do study comparative religion, not only may there be non-Christian students who listen to a foreigner expounding their own faith, but there are increasingly members of those faiths who speak of what religion really means to them. An outstanding instance is at McGill university, where the departments of Comparative Religion and Islamic Studies are under a Christian head but at least half of the staff is Muslim. Advanced students here are required to spend some time in the Arab world, and doctorates must not only satisfy western academic standards but also be acceptable within the Islamic tradition.

It is right that a religion should be studied in its own context. It is also right that there should be over-all studies of several religions, and not only of particular faiths. If the truth can be spoken in love, and that dialogue be begun between the religions that was lacking in the past, then it may be possible for an outsider to understand what it feels like to be a Hindu, or a Buddhist, from within. How does Islam look, not to the Christian, but to the Muslim? To know this leads to understanding its motive-power. But only men of faith can answer these questions, so that the comparative study of religions demands a stronger rather than a weaker faith.

This strong faith in turn may find that other religions are our allies, and confound the fears of the timorous who are nervous of dabbling in religions. One is asked at times whether by studying other religions one's own faith is not undermined. This assumes that the religions are in conflict, but if they can be allies then the situation is changed. The answer to the question then is that study of other religions, as faiths men live by, can deepen and strengthen one's own faith. To know something of the devotion of the Muslim's five daily prayers, the long and arduous discipline of Hindu yoga, the self-control and concentration of Buddhist meditation, can be a great stimulus to the lagging zeal of Christian prayer and spiritual training.

Toynbee writes of the help that can come from seeing others engaged in the same quest for reality but along different paths. 'The fact that I and my neighbour are following different roads is something that divides us much less than we are drawn together by the other fact that, in following our different roads, we are both trying to approach the same mystery. All human beings who are seeking to approach the mystery in order to direct their lives in accordance with the nature and spirit of Absolute Reality or, in theistic terms, with the will of God—all these fellow-seekers are engaged in an identical quest. They should recognize that they are spiritually brethren and should feel towards one another, and treat one another, as such.'[9]

[9] *An Historian's Approach to Religion*, p. 251.

CHAPTER 6

PROBLEMS OF PROPAGANDA

Dialogue between the religions is not made easier by the fact that some of them seek to convert others to their own faith. Some of the world's greatest religions have been missionary faiths from the outset, believing that the truths they held are available for all men, independently of caste, race or colour. Others have arisen and remained largely as national faiths, into which men are born and from which they cannot depart except at the risk of social stigmas. Even some of these, however, have been stimulated into forms of missionary activity by the example of other propagating faiths.

Hinduism is a great national growth, and like most indigenous religions it did not look beyond its own frontiers. Its comprehensive outlook permitted the rise of sects, such as Jainism and Buddhism, which were universal and not bound to caste. But if Brahmins were to leave their religion there was often a great disturbance; the renegade would be expelled and treated as an outcaste Parangi.

The Parsis, owing to their troubled history, became closed in upon themselves as a national community. They teach that each man should follow the religion into which he was born, and theirs today is the only religion in the world which forbids members of another faith to enter any of its temples.

Judaism also, despite its great universalist prophets, no longer seeks to extend its faith outside the membership of its own race. Rabbi Epstein said recently that 'when paganism gave place to Christianity and later also to Islam, Judaism withdrew from the missionary field and was satisfied to leave the task of spreading the religion of humanity to her daughter faiths.'[1]

Three great religions, Christianity, Islam and Buddhism, have always been missionary in principle, although at some periods they have been content with ground gained without

1 *Judaism*, 1959, p. 144.

seeking to extend it. Jainism and Sikhism have also been missionary in principle, but in fact have been confined to small numbers, in race or caste.

It is difficult for the missionary faiths to explain to the non-missionary what right they think they have to proselytize, and it is often hard enough for them to understand themselves what are the limits and methods of propagation. In modern times both methods and limits are likely to be carefully examined and criticized as examples of empire-building, perhaps even on the political plane. In the olden days it was often said that the faith followed the flag, and was an instrument of imperialism. There was enough truth in this to make it sting.

If the object of the mission is to supplant, and eventually completely destroy the religion attacked, then the reaction of the latter is understandable. This is sometimes stated explicitly, though often enough it is simply implicit. Thus an Anglican writer says that the primary purpose of the Christian mission must be 'to abolish all other religions of the world'. A Roman Catholic admits that 'the practical consequences of dogmatic intolerance, for example, the efforts to win the whole world and supplant all other religions, also have an unpleasant effect in Asia.[2] Hence Rabindranath Tagore objected that if ever mankind were to be swallowed up by one single form of religion, God would have to provide another Noah's ark to save man from the annihilation of his soul. The real threat of this danger from Communism is now apparent.

The temptation to attack and misrepresent a religion is very great, for propaganda is always in danger of using exaggeration. Mahatma Gandhi, though later deeply influenced by certain Christian teachings, told how he disliked it in his youth. 'And for a reason. In those days Christian missionaries used to stand in a corner near the high school and hold forth, pouring abuse on Hindus and their gods . . . About the same time I heard of a well-known Hindu having been converted to Christianity. It was the talk of the town that when he was baptized, he had to

[2] C. J. Shebbeare, *Christianity and Other Religions* (1939), p. 13; Ohm, *op. cit.*, p. 39.

eat beef and drink liquor, that he also had to change his clothes, and that henceforth he began to go about in European costume including a hat . . . I also heard that the new convert had already begun abusing the religion of his ancestors, their customs and their country,'[3] That many of these criticisms do not bear on real Christianity, and could not be made today, is part of the real objection.

Because of his experiences Gandhi urged that people should respect all religions, and not leave their own for another. 'No one religion can really be proved to be better than any other. But it is best for a man to follow more faithfully the precepts and practices of the religion in which he has been brought up. Therefore no one should try to carry on any organized propaganda to further the claims of any religion, especially if such propaganda involves proselytism. On the other hand, every attempt should be made to help people develop an attitude of respect for all religions, a willingness to know about other religions and to accept what is good in all of them.'

Hindu nationalists since Gandhi's day have gone further, and some would not only forbid all missionary work but would make all other religious communities subordinate to the Hindu. The Rāshtriya Sevak Sangh declares that only the Hindu race and culture should be glorified, and that non-Hindu peoples should have no privileges, not even citizenship rights. But these are extremists, and the Indian republic is a secular state, guaranteeing freedom to all religions.

A more moderate Hindu point of view is given by D. S. Sarma when he says, 'Our policy should be one not of absorption but of fraternization. In this great country all of us have to live in peace, each community following its own *Dharma*. Islam and Christianity will, no doubt, insist on their rights of propaganda and conversion. We cannot quarrel with them on that ground, so long as they do not employ force or unfair means to compass their object.' But a new note appears in a further sentence, which shows that the missionizing spirit has entered into Hinduism. 'We must, of course, claim the same rights and freely take into our fold not only all those who once belonged to it and want to

[3] *An Autobiography*, p. 24f.

come back to it, but also those who are born in other faiths, but want to embrace Hinduism.'[4]

So the national religion seeks internationalism, and one consequence of missionary propaganda is that the faith attacked turns round and itself takes to proselytizing Hinduism should become more credal, says Sarma, to give it authority and coherence. With its many schools there is no need for rigidity, but when a man has chosen the path that suits him he should conform to its rituals and usages faithfully. In like manner the Rāmakrishna Mission sets forth its version of universal Hinduism or syncretism, and movements like the Arya Samāj and the Hindu Mahāsabhā seek to protect Hindus from missionaries and win back those who have gone over to other religions.

Where two dogmatic and missionary religions face one another acute problems are raised. There was much acrimony in past days, on the part of Christian and Muslim governments, and in modern times imperial rulers have tried to hold the scales between missions from either side. The British government in East and West Africa purported to be the protector of Islam, to the detriment of Christian missionaries. No churches could be built in Kano or Omdurman, no missionary could ever enter British Somaliland and no portion of the Bible was ever allowed to be circulated there. The ban on Christian missionaries in Northern Nigeria did not prevent the Muslims there from spreading their faith among the largely Christian peoples to the south; they took their religion seriously, believing every man to have a right to it.

Government administrators have been known to defend restriction of missionary teaching by saying that conversion was dangerous, or even unnecessary for the people, 'their religion is good enough for them.' If this implies a racial superiority, so that some can enjoy the best but others must be content with the second-best, then no truly religious man would defend this for he believes every man to have a right to the best.

But the right to conversion is criticized on other grounds, which deserve more careful and imaginative consideration

[4] *Hinduism through the Ages*, pp. 276f.

than is often given to them. Freedom of religion is one of the fundamental freedoms for which we have fought. It implies also freedom to change one's religion, on sincere conviction, and without undue pressure from any side. But even so objections can be raised.

It is not possible to understand the objections that have been raised to conversion until we put ourselves in the place of other people. That somebody is taken from his religion and becomes a member of our own may appear legitimate proselytization. But what if it happens in reverse? If a Christian becomes a Muslim or a Buddhist, how do Christians feel? Do they think, he has denied Christ? With all the ingrained horror that that implies. Then perhaps it may be possible to understand the feelings of Victor Gollancz who, attracted by Christianity, but far more by Christ, and contemplating baptism, then drew back. 'I was the sort of Jew, and remain one, who in the presence of antisemitism regards formal apostasy as disgusting . . . Finally, there was my father. He had been horribly wounded by my sister's conversion: could I wound him again still more horribly—for I was his son, not his daughter—without being sure, at the very least without being sure, that my motives were unmixed and that what I had contemplated was inexorably demanded by conscience?'[5]

And here is a Muslim who has become critical of certain statements and ideas in the sacred Qur'ān. Christians have been critical of the Bible over the last hundred years, though that was thought to be a dreadful attitude in the last century. But faith in the verbal inspiration of the Bible has gone from many Christian circles, for not the Bible but Christ himself is the Word of God. Similar criticism of the Qur'ān is yet to come. But this Muslim is so concerned about it that eventually he leaves Islam and becomes a Christian. But some say that this is a pity, for he thereby prevents at once any further influence of his ideas working upon his erstwhile fellows, since they now regard him as a traitor to the faith.

Further, this same Muslim, because he lived in America, became even more isolated and had great difficulty in entering into the Christian community which differs so widely

[5] *My dear Timothy*, p. 414.

in race and tradition from his own. There are frequent complaints from converts that they have become wanderers, not belonging to any society. 'In Kuala Lumpur an important Indian merchant complained that in spite of his social position and his membership of the Church he found it impossible to enter white society. Similar complaints are often voiced. The convert to Islam finds himself at once on a par with other Moslems. Christians, however, rarely regard and treat the Asian Christians as their brothers in Christ.'[6] This applies to European Christians, not of course to Asian or African.

Without conversion many Muslims have come to read and appreciate much of the Bible, and have a better understanding of Christ than in the past. Islam has always recognized the prominent place of Christ, and honours him as Prophet, Messiah, and sinless. But there is more knowledge about him today, and especially of his teaching of which the Qur'ān says virtually nothing. Several outstanding Muslim lives of Jesus have appeared in recent years, especially in Egypt where the ending of the old imperialism has shown the distinction between Christianity and imperialism. These lives show a close acquaintance with the Gospels and a sympathetic understanding of the great moments in the life of Christ. Abbas al-Aqqad has written on *The Genius of Christ*, Abd al Sahhar on *Jesus the Christ*, and Muhammad Khalid in 1958 published his *Muhammad and Christ on the Road Together*, in which the Qur'ān and the Sermon on the Mount are linked in an appeal for social justice and world peace. But the most striking of all is Kamel Hussein's *City of Wrong*, which makes a close examination and reconstruction of the people and their motives in the events of Good Friday. These are all men who have remained Muslims while studying the central fact of Christianity.

Christian missions in Muslims lands have produced few converts, for so often they have proceeded by head-on attack. Often they knew nothing of the religion, or even the language, of the people they tried to convert. One has even heard it said that Communism should come in to destroy the religion, so as to leave place for a fresh start for mis-

[6] Ohm, *op. cit.*, p. 61f.

sions. But this is a shocking attitude, a denial of our common faith in God, of the great values of Muslim culture, and a foolish assumption that Communism would allow new and usually fundamentalist missions to rival its sway. Surely a better way is growth of the knowledge of Christ among Muslims, and even the encouragement of Christian Muslims.

In many Buddhist lands the situation is similar. There are very few converts from Buddhism, and dialogue to understand Buddhism has hardly begun. Cathedrals and churches present a western form of religion, with formal liturgies and canticles transliterated. The graceful native pagodas are still thronged with people to whom their traditional religion clearly makes the greatest appeal.

By dialogue between the faiths, light may be accepted from other sources, and in their turn these religions may help to bring fresh insights into Christian faith, and certainly give a much-needed stimulus to devotion. The unity of God has been the great emphasis of Islam, but this is Christian belief also. 'We cannot proceed except on the understanding that we are both firmly and equally believers that God is One. We both stand squarely in the Hebrew tradition: "The Lord our Lord is ONE Lord." We are not discussing theism and tritheism. Christianity is concerned only with the first. Muslims who debate tritheism are not discussing Christianity. Where we differ is over how to define and understand the Divine Unity.'[7]

In days gone by a Muslim criticism of Christian teaching was over the term 'Son' used of Jesus. This originated from Muhammad's attack on the pagan deities of Mecca who had been called sons and daughters of Allah. The idea of physical sonship and paternity applied literally to God was rightly abhorrent to the Prophet. Only now after many centuries is it possible to discuss this concept calmly and to discover that we both reject the notion of physical begetting by God. The Christian finds it necessary to insist to Muslims that 'the expression "Son of God" excludes all paternity in a physical sense. On Christian premises the latter is unthinkable'. And so the Muslim can now reply that 'Muslims do

[7] K. Cragg, *The Call of the Minaret* (1956), p. 308.

not object if the term *son* is used in an allegorical sense'.[8] The idea of God can be enriched, and Christian teaching saved from excessive anthropomorphism, if these things are understood. Both Islam and Christianity have a witness to bear to one another, which is only hindered by ignorant propaganda.

In devotional practices attempts have been made to adapt yoga exercises to Christian needs. This was worth trying, if only in view of the widespread appeal of yoga to the West. How far efforts have been successful in taking methods of self-control and grafting them on to prayers to God, may be doubted. One of the best known adapters deliberately rejects the whole Hindu context of thought, and seeks the redemption of the body and the development of meditation and concentration in an entirely Christian atmosphere. This can be done, and it may also be remembered that Hindu yoga is very frequently a means of devotion to God, as well as being used in a non-theistic context.[9]

The indirect influence of faiths upon one another is very great nowadays, and cannot be denied. Many people come within the cultural sway of another religion without abandoning their own. Mahatma Gandhi was an outstanding example of this. His famous doctrine of non-violence (ahimsā) was derived from Janism and from Tolstoy and the Sermon on the Mount, rediscovering a truth which Christianity had almost forgotten. The deepest level of Christianity is the Cross, so often a stumbling-block to both Jews and Gentiles. Yet when Gandhi was in prison it was his friend, the missionary C. F. Andrews, who visited him and sang at his request the hymn, 'When I survey the wondrous Cross'. And when Gandhi was assassinated, and cremated on the banks of the Jumna outside Delhi, in those vast plains where it is said literally millions of people gathered together, as the funeral pyre was lit those Hindus heard a small group singing this Christian hymn.

The house of a friend in Calcutta, a member of the Brāhmo Samāj, has a room on the walls of which are tablets

[8] *ibid.*, p. 291. And S. M. Tufail, 'Bridging the Gulf between Islam and Christianity', in *Forum*, (June 1960).

[9] See J. M. Déchanet, *Christian Yoga* (1960).

bearing inscribed texts from many of the world's great religions. There each verse seeks to give the essence of Greek and Roman, Hindu and Buddhist, Taoist and Muslim, Jewish and Christian faiths. From the Greek comes 'Know thyself'; from the Latin, 'I am a man, nothing human is foreign to me'; from Sanskrit, 'That thou art'; from Buddhism, 'Hail to the Jewel in the Lotus'; from Chinese, 'The sage relies on actionless activity'; from the Qur'ān, 'In the name of God, the Merciful, the Compassionate'; and from the Old Testament, 'Love thy neighbour as thyself'. What from Christianity? What verse could be singled out giving the essence of the faith? The one chosen is that dreadful verse from St Mark's Gospel, 'My God, my God, why hast thou forsaken me?' Yet in that choice this Hindu has perceived the heart of what Christianity has tried to set out as its message to the sufferings of mankind. Apparently it is not necessary always to be a convert in order to understand the deepest truths of another religion.

The future methods of missions will need to be different from those of the past. Some lands will only permit them if their methods are without force and bribery. There will be no hiding under a foreign flag, the missions must be acceptable by their own works. They must no longer denounce or despise the gods and scriptures of other peoples. They must practise true charity in word and deed.

If the right of freedom of religion is invoked, with the corollary of the right to change one's religion, then the same right will be claimed for missions to Europe and America.

Europeans cannot reasonably object to the proselytizing Buddhist, Muslim and Rāmakrishna societies in their midst. They might even welcome rivalry, as a stimulus to deeper knowledge of the teachings and ascetic practices of their own faith. The presence of practising members of other religions in our midst may serve to revive devotion, and serious dialogue may lead to revival of faith in the West, as the presence of missions in the East has often stimulated Asian religions to new life.

'In all things charity', must be the aim of those who deal in spiritual things. Baron von Hügel, the Roman Catholic theologian, once said, 'with regard to non-Christian religions and as to how fervent Christians can respect these religions at their best, I love to think of Cardinal de Lavigerie, the zealous Missionary Archbishop—of his alighting from his carriage and proceeding on foot past such Mosques as he happened to pass in his Algerian Diocese'. Would that this charity and respect had always been observed by missionaries for the holy places of other religions.

Not only must there be respect for buildings, but also for religious beliefs. It used to be common enough for missionaries to ridicule or misrepresent the teachings of other religions, instead of respecting them as genuine efforts at apprehending spiritual reality. And during leave at home the missionary on money-raising deputation tours often spoke in harsh terms of other religions. This is increasingly difficult today when so many laymen have been to the East and know something of its temples.

So an Indian Christian appeals that 'evangelism should avoid all methods of propaganda which fall into the temptation of exaggerating the validity of Christian claims by deliberately minimizing the inherent worth of other faiths. The past history of Christian evangelism in India has unfortunately given room for such a charge. We have painted in dark colours the grim side of Hindu religious beliefs and practices, and not given sufficient recognition to the values that are of intrinsic worth in Hindu life and thought. Especially is this true of descriptions we have given about the Hindu and his religion to people of other lands. Perhaps the missionary has been the greatest culprit in this regard. With the best intention we have frequently misjudged the faiths of others, and it is well that we now make amends for some of the wrongs that we have committed.'[10]

Congregations in Europe used to sing of Ceylon's isle where 'only man is vile', and that 'the heathen in his blindness bows down to wood and stone'. Today these verses are usually omitted, out of respect for the Ceylonese, and because no 'heathen' ever bows down to wood and stone but worships the spirit represented by these images. But children may still be taught to sing of 'lands where Islam's sway

[10] P. D. Devanandan, *The Gospel and Renascent Hinduism*, (1959), p. 33.

darkly broods o'er hearth and home', and similar sweeping condemnations. There is too great a temptation for the missionary advocate to enliven his appeal by painting a black picture of ignorance, idolatry and oppression. Similar dark descriptions could be given of Roman Catholic Sicily and Colombia, or Calvinist South Africa.

Confusion must not be made between faith and practice, nor between social and religious wrongs. Many Hindus, as well as Christians, are shocked by the blood sacrifices in the temples of Kālī in Calcutta. Dr Radhakrishnan expresses his regret that the reformer Shankara in the ninth century was not able to reform the Kalighat. 'He put down the grosser manifestations of the Shākta worship in South India, and it is a pity that his influence is not discernible in the great temple of Kālī in Calcutta.'[11]

There are many social reforms which are now taking place that take the sting out of past criticism. Gandhi did far more than anyone else for the removal of untouchability in India, and the abuses of polygamy are being checked today by Muslims themselves in many lands. Such reforms receive too little mention in missionary propaganda. Criticism is still directed at the lowly state of women, often not so lowly and thought by many Asians to show greater purity than in the lax morals of the West. But it is not so long since Christian Europe was stirred at last to emancipate women, by suffragette movements and property laws. And women are still banned from the ministry of most churches, although they provide the church's strongest support.

Appreciation of what other faiths teach, and of the good and helpful in them, and a desire 'not to destroy but to fulfil', would be suitable for missionary workers. And national Christians who have adopted a new faith should not break with the good in their country's past. The father of a friend who was converted to Christianity burnt all his Sanskrit books in the zeal of a new faith. But his son, though a Christian, made great efforts to learn Sanskrit, and delights in its literature, especially that of the devotional *bhakti* cults.

'For some unaccountable reason,' says Devandandan,

[11] *Indian Philosophy*, i, p. 450.

'Christians in India have neglected to cultivate a scholarly acquaintance with the creed, cultus and culture of Hinduism at its many levels of outreach, in terms both of its scriptural bases and as supported by the sanctions of tradition. Two generations ago it was different. Christian scholars were then regarded as authorities in the field, and though not all of them produced works of lasting interest, some of their excellent translations of Hindu classics and their painstaking efforts to establish reliable historical data for the study of Hinduism continue to be of substantial value.'[12] A minority of the older missionaries did study the Sanskrit and other classics. Many others did not. There are few modern authorities of equal calibre with the best of the past. And Indian Christians by neglecting the literature and art of the past have cut themselves off from the cultural renaissance which is a feature of modern India. In doing so they risk defeating their own purpose and becoming an enclosed community or caste, fossilized as the Syrian Church of Malabar was for centuries.

A living religion should inspire the culture of the country, it should assist in reforms of social evils, and pioneer in the creation of new ways of life and worship. 'Christians find that in rendering service they necessarily need to collaborate with men of other faiths or no faith. This calls for a measure of identification with those who do not agree with us.'[13] This is in the social sphere. In religious matters the communications between religions which have been opened today, make it possible to regard other faiths not as utterly wrong, or purely subservient, but as all contributing to a deeper understanding of truth.

[12] *op. cit.*, p. 55.
[13] Devanandan, *op cit.*, p. 59.

CHAPTER 7

SYNCRETISM OR ADAPTATION?

When Sir Francis Younghusband initiated the first meetings which led to the formation of the World Congress of Faiths, in 1936, they were said by their critics to aim at the amalgamation of all religions. This organization now has the support of members of many faiths, some of them very eminent: such as the Dean of St Paul's, Dr. Bentwich, and Professor Radhakrishnan. But they were suspected of being so concerned with the unity of religions as to be working towards a unification, in which the distinctive elements of each faith would be submerged in an amorphous whole.

Because of this fear an official declaration was made by the World Congress, which appears in every issue of its journal, stating that: 'It in no way attempts to exalt one faith at the expense of another nor does it seek to formulate a new amalgamated creed.'

There is no doubt that this disclaimer is necessary, and that there are strong tendencies abroad towards adopting elements from any religion, regarding all as of equal value, and moving towards a synthetic religion. Gandhi declared that 'essentially all religions are the same', and the conclusion is often drawn that therefore they may be freely merged into one another.

In academic works the effort at syncretism is well illustrated by the writings of Frithjof Schuon, and especially in *The Transcendent Unity of Religions*. Here he maintains that there is 'metaphysical' truth which is one, and 'religious' truths which are many and different manifestations of the inexpressible metaphysical truth. This is rather mystifying, for if the metaphysical truth is inexpressible it is difficult to know what any religion or philosophy can say about it. But perhaps more important is the fact that Schuon is hardly charitable in confining religious truth to orthodoxy, or consistent in then proceeding to dismiss Protestantism as heresy while admitting Shī'a Islam and Buddhism as orthodoxies. However, perhaps his attempt to show the essential unity of religions was worth making, as Zaehner comments, if only because it shows that such unity is hard to achieve.

There are many other notable writers on similar lines, the most outstanding being Radhakrishnan who in his commentaries on the Vedānta quotes many European writers side by side with Indian to show likeness of expression, or possibility of borrowing, syncretism already made in the past: 'From the mystical doctrines of the Upanishads, one current of thought may be traced in the mysticism of the Persian Sufism, to the mystic, theosophical logos doctrine of the Neo-Platonics and the Alexandrian Christian mystics, Eckhart and Tauler, and finally to the philosophy of the great German mystic of the nineteenth century, Schopenhauer.'[1] The last named at least is unfortunate, for Schopenhauer was so obsessed with the Upanishads that he thought that all other religious truth came from there and even the New Testament must be traceable to an Indian source; 'its ethical system, its ascetic view or morality, its pessimism, and its Avatar, are all thoroughly Indian.'

The Neo-Vedāntin school whose best known western representatives are Aldous Huxley, Christopher Isherwood, and Gerald Heard, brings more material to the work of synthesis. But like so many syntheses it tends to put forward claims to provide a substitute for older faiths. So it is said that, 'A new religion has come into history—that is Western Vedanta . . . the appearance of Vedanta in the West as a living religion, and not as an academic study, is inevitable just because the religious heredity of the West has now outgrown the tight Hebrew pot of cosmology in which it had been growing for two millenia. A faith that taught hell for those who did not get themselves saved in this life was suited enough to put the fear of God into barbarians or into men too busy to do much more than make a dash with their last breath for a deathbed repentance. But for people really interested in the spiritual world, really desirous of growing in spirituality and filled with a longing to know and love God, such doctrines were, far from being any help, a terrible obstacle.'[2]

1 *The Principal Upanishads*, p. 18n.
2 G. Heard in *Vedanta for Modern Man* (Allen & Unwin, 1952), p. 1f.

Most of the Neo-Vedāntic movement stems from Rāmakrishna, and some from theosophy. Both these influences arose in the nineteenth century, and sought to prove the unity of religions, but under strong Hindu influence. Rāmakrishna gave a great deal of thought to the problem of the diversity of religions, so apparent in India down the ages and made more acute in the last century by the missionary activity of European Christians. 'God is one but his aspects are many,' he said, 'one God is worshipped in different countries and ages, and has different forms and names.' He used the ancient and famous illustration of the four blind men and the elephant, each man describing it differently from the member that he touched. 'In the same manner those quarrel who have seen one aspect only of the Deity.' So all paths lead to the truth, nevertheless, every man should follow his own religion.'

The Rāmakrishna mission was founded in 1897, under the inspiration of Vivekānanda. In its declared aims the Mission looks upon 'all religions as paths to God'. But it engages in widespread missionary activity to further the aims of the Mission. Its principal temple, at Belur, Calcutta, is a deliberate attempt at a synthesis, combining Hindu, Buddhist and Muslim motifs in its architecture, while in the main shrine sits a marble image of Rāmakrishna in the place occupied by the chief deity of Hindu temples and receiving similar gifts from worshippers.

In the recognition of other faiths and names of God, Rāmakrishna was following a path traced by Kabir, Nānak, and the Sikhs four centuries earlier. And like the Mission the Sikh religion is a clear and confessed synthesis, only with a much stronger infusion of Muslim monotheism. The Sikhs claim that Guru Nānak found that 'the misery of the people was their disunity born of diversity of belief'. He sought, therefore, to bring together Muslim and Hindu beliefs and make a religion of deliberate synthesis. The Sikh scriptures, the Ādi Granth, include impartially hymns written by Hindus and Muslims. However, there was a strong missionary emphasis in the religion, and in time the Sikh community became a tightly knit brotherhood, through the pressure of persecution and the binding force of vows of initiation.

Almost contemporary with Rāmakrishna, but in the Muslim environment of Persia (a land however which has undergone the influence of many religions, and the home of the Sūfī mystics with their broad spirit), lived the Bāb, the new prophet of the Bahā'ī religion founded by his follower Bahā'u'llah. The Bahā'ī religion recognizes other religions, but claims to complete them. Muhammad is accepted as the 'seal of the prophets', but the last prophet in the Age of Promise. Now the Bāb has closed that past age and opened the present Age of Fulfilment. Once again a syncretistic religion turns to missionary activity to convert men of other faiths to its own membership.

A religion of synthesis, however, is not the only possible result of recognizing the good in other religions. It has been tried, with varying success. But other attitudes are possible, and are held in fact by large numbers of people in other religions. Many leading Muslims, in all ages, have seen some truth in Judaism and Christianity, but have not been less convinced and devout Muslims for that.

W. E. Hocking, in his *Living Religions and a World Faith*, discussed the case for synthesis of religions, and pointed out that it may be of more than one kind. Early Islam adopted practices from pagan Arabia, but so covered them with new meaning that the pagan signification was lost. The pilgrimage to Mecca, the circumlocution of the Ka'ba (deliberately changed by Muhammad to the anti-clockwise direction), visits to sacred hills and sacrificing sheep, all were given a full Muslim context and have so remained to this day. In like manner Gregory the Great, Bede tells us, instructed the missionaries to pagan Britain not to destroy the native temples but 'let holy water be made and sprinkled in the said temples, let altars be erected and relics put there', so that the people 'may the more familiarly resort to the places to which they have been accustomed'. All religions, in fact, have inherited customs and beliefs from those among which they grew up. Our Christmas and Easter customs: mistletoe, holly, tree, hot-cross buns, Easter eggs, and the like, were all pagan and some of them fertility rites; but they have all been baptized into Christianity. In other places, such as South America, so many of the old customs have remained that they threaten to cover or distort Christianity but this faith is still comparatively new there.

Deliberate synthesis, by the leaders of a religion, may be of great value. The adoption of the word Allah for the sole God was of great help to the Muslims among the polytheistic Arabs. Christian missions have often taken a native name for God, and in China have used the concept of Tao, the 'way' or 'doctrine' as a near-equivalent of the Logos; 'in the beginning was Tao.' But this is very different from careless synthesis in which uninformed worshippers retain or adopt any and every idol that pleases them.

Hocking regards the better ways of synthesis as preparatory to his own idea of re-conception. In this a new faith will take up the values of an old one and transform them, thus producing a new creation. This is regarded as the natural process of religious growth, whereby a religion builds deliberately on the foundation of another, say Christianity on Hinduism, incorporates its noblest aspects, and produces a new and higher Christianity. This is attractive, though there is the suggestion that one religion only has value in so far as it subserves another. Hinduism deserves study in its own right, yet it may be asked whether a Christian can ever understand it without any influence of his own religion. Certainly as J. H. Newman said, it is difficult to belong to two religions at once, and quite impossible to be what Dean Inge called 'an honorary member of all religions'.

The notion that all religions are of equal truth and value is one of the commonest misconceptions. It is often assumed that a student of other religions, who admits truth in them, must agree that all religions are the same. All roads lead to the goal, all rivers flow to the sea, so all faiths are equal paths to the truth, and there is no reason to change one's religion; nor, one might suppose, to receive light from any other religion.

The Japanese have a proverb: 'Every road leads to its end. Every religion is good. Do not various roads lead up to Mt

Fuji?'[3] This is understandable perhaps in Japan where for a thousand years the great experiment of Ryōbu Shinto, mixed Shinto and Buddhism, flourished; though Buddhism held the upper hand, until the Shinto reaction in the nineteenth century. But recent years have seen an ever increasing number of Shinto and Buddhist sects, most of which are syncretistic, with a strong infusion of Christian ways too.

But if one thing is striking in the comparative study of religions, it is the diversity of religion, and the different levels at which it is manifested. The very multiplicity of sects and schools in every religion is surprising, and is even reassuring to a Christian tired of the jangling sects of his own religion. Clearly all religions are not the same. But can one discriminate between them?

It is, as has been said earlier, a precarious affair to set up standards between the religions, or to judge one by another. Yet everyone has some standards which are set by his faith. It is hard for a monotheist to think of polytheism as an equal way with his own, or for a Muslim or Quaker to appreciate the use of images in worship. Some religions have a stronger appeal because of their many points of kinship, in doctrine and ethic, with one's own. But there are religions or sects which have had degraded and immoral rites. The World Congress of Faiths wished to invite all religions to its first meetings, but refused to accept tribes that might still practise human sacrifice or temple prostitution. If all religions are equal, then the human sacrifices of the ancient Peruvians and the murderous robberies of the Thugs must rank with the teaching of the Sermon on the Mount.

It is usually agreed that there has been development in religion, as in human culture generally. Progress is not inevitable, and degeneration is common, but clear stages of progress can be observed. Although religion is very old, traces of it being found from Paleolithic times at least, yet there have been crises and periods of great development. Reformers have arisen who have purged away unworthy practices, and have set up new standards. Is their work to be denied, under the claim that all forms of religion are

[3] Ohm, *op. cit.*, p. 25.

equal? The great sixth century B.C., when lived the Buddha, Mahāvīra, Zoroaster, Confucius, Lao Tsu, Heraclitus, Jeremiah and the Second Isaiah, has often been hailed as such a time when religion took great strides forward, inspired by outstanding geniuses. It would hardly be said that illiterate animists, whose religion has no trace of great prophets and no line of sacred scripture, have such a high religion as those who follow what are commonly called the Great Religions.

And in the 'higher' religion, as has been said elsewhere, each claims certain unique elements. The Hindu believes in God, either personal or impersonal, and in an immortal soul; the Buddhist believes in neither. The Semitic religions believe in judgement after death and resurrection to eternal life, the Indian faiths hold to reincarnation and final nirvāna. These unique elements cannot be easily dissipated, and it is really quite misleading to say, as Tagore did, that 'fundamentally Christ preached exactly the same message as Buddha'.

Because of the unique elements, faith in Christ or the Qur'ān, members of each religion will continue to regard their own faith as superior, even when ready to recognize truths in other religions. Indeed not to do so would seem to demand changing one's religion, for the other one that now appears as superior. This is how the process of religious conversion comes about. And it has been the logic of the synthetic religions that has led them to set up as superior faiths over all others. It is still quite practicable, however, for a member of any religion to admit the good in other faiths, and the failings of his own, and yet to hold firmly to the uniqueness of his own religion.

It is strange that some of the open synthesizers of religion, and those who think all religions are of equal truth, regard it as a grave error on the part of others not to agree to their point of view. The convinced Christian or Muslim is told to abandon his narrow viewpoint and join boldly in a theosophical free-for-all in which praises are heaped on some of the most dubious creeds, and questionably moral practices are justified, because all are divine and therefore all are true.

Not only this, but the further conclusion is drawn that

religions which cling obstinately to their own particular creed, without merging it fully in the general pool, are blind and prejudiced. It is claimed, as E. L. Allen notes, 'that the religions that acknowledge all to be on the same level are *ipso facto* on a higher level than the others.'[4] All religions are equal, but some are more equal than others.

If great care has to be taken not to confuse different elements of religion, or bring all down to a dead level, are there not experiments that can be made to bridge the gulf that separates faith from faith? Indeed there are, as has been insisted. Dialogue between religions is urgent, with the confrontation of religions today. Only now have meetings become possible where men can speak, as men of religion and positive faith, to others of different creeds but like concern for spiritual things. The Council for Christians and Jews has existed since 1923 and has done much valuable work. As a result of a meeting in the Lebanon a Continuing Committee on Muslim-Christian Co-operation was set up in 1954. And further conversations by Muslims, Jews, Christians and Druzes have taken place, significantly, in Jerusalem. In the academic sphere the Union for the Study of the Great Religions, and the International Association for the History of Religions, have done much to further the study of religions and bring together scholars of different faiths.

Gandhi said that 'More than all, people of all religions should learn to worship together on occasion'. This would appear more difficult but experiments continue to be made. In North Africa, under the guidance of the great French scholar Louis Massignon, Muslims and Christians have shared retreats and gone on pilgrimages together. In China, Karl Reichelt opened monasteries to which Buddhists and Confucians came to meditate with Christians. In India āshrams have been opened by Christians as well as Hindus for common worship. And the World Congress of Faiths has an annual service in London at which a Muslim imām, a Jewish rabbi, a Buddhist monk, a Sikh leader, and a Nonconformist minister may read passages from their own scriptures and meditate together in an Anglican church. No

[4] *op. cit.*, p. 122.

doubt the whole matter is surrounded with difficulties, but it is essential that religion should not be regarded simply as an object of study like any secular affair, but a faith of persons. This faith needs not only to be described by outsiders but seen in the worshipping activity of those who hold it.

If a syncretistic religion is not desirable, yet it is possible that there are elements in other religions which may be borrowed. This has been tried by European students of yoga, but not often in a Christian context or discerning the religious doctrines and attitudes implied in it. Yet devotional practices can serve western religions well. Protestant churches, even more than Roman Catholic, have neglected meditation and concentration to their great impoverishment. If the West can teach social reform and ecclesiastical organization to the East (for example in Parsi societies, or Buddhist Sunday schools and choirs), the East in turn can display great effort expended on devotion, on the discipline and cultivation of the spiritual life.

Attempts have been made from time to time to adopt some of the eastern religious classics into Christian use. The Old Testament has been a problem for the churches, not only in Europe but even more in Asia. Some parts of it are frankly barbaric (e.g. Psalm 137) and others quite out of touch with Indian and Far Eastern life. So it has been suggested that selections from the Vedāntic literature can be adopted as a sort of Ethnic Old Testament, in India, and similarly from other scriptures elsewhere. The Old Testament is implied in so much of the New, however, that it is not possible to dispense with it altogether. As in England the revised lectionaries give selections from what are plainly purple passages, so the same process has been followed elsewhere. Readings from other scriptures are then taken as alternatives or supplements. There too selections are made, but have been taken fairly widely.

Christian āshrams have used classic Hindu expressions of devotion, so as to root worship in an indigenous setting. 'We held daily worship during the morning and evening twilight periods, known as sandhya, the "joints" of night and day, and set apart by long usage in India for meditation and prayer. At these times we would assemble in the open air and sit in a semi-circle, facing in the morning towards the deepening glory of the sunrise and in the evening towards the slow-fading sunset . . . Then the leader would bid those present to lift their hearts to Christ, the true light, and all together would recite in Sanskrit the *Gayatri Mantra,* that ancient invocation by repetition of which the Hindu concentrates his spirit for contemplation of the Eternal: "Let us meditate on the excellent glory of the Divine Illuminer. May He inspire our understanding!" Then would follow a deep silence of corporate meditation, like that of a Quaker meeting; at the end of which all would join in the familiar Sanskrit prayer:

From the unreal lead me to the Real:
From darkness lead me to light:
From death lead me to immortality;

and then the soft chant: *shanti* (*peace*)*; shanti; shanti.*'[5]

Many such experiments have been tried, with greater or lesser success and duration. In the realm of doctrinal borrowing, at least, we are apt to suffer from our friends. The western Neo-Vedāntin advocates of exchanges between religions, freely adopting concepts like nirvāna or an impersonal divine, without reflecting sufficiently on their coherence with traditional western patterns of belief, serve to repel other westerners from comparative religion.

But that some exchanges between religions have taken place is certain, and such cross-fertilization can be of great profit. Scholars generally agree that belief in the resurrection of the dead and a future judgement came from Zoroastrianism into Judaism at a late period. There is no trace of such beliefs in the early Old Testament literature, but they appear clearly in the late book of Daniel (written about the second century B.C.). Thence these beliefs developed in later Judaism, in Christianity and Islam. Other concepts of demons and angels from similar sources were perhaps less happy, though no less potent importations. In like manner Zaehner has shown that the idea of union with

[5] J. C. Winslow, *The Christian Approach to the Hindu* (1958), p. 55f.

God, foreign to early Islam, came to the Persian Sūfīs from India, through Al-Sindī and Abū Yazīd, and was popularized by Hallāj. It was centuries before this idea was widely accepted in Islam, and some people may think it unfortunate, but there is no doubt of its later wide influence in true Islamic circles.

If indiscriminate syncretism is rejected, yet there may still be valuable influences and fertilization between religions. Some would hold that these are essential to the West, if the near-bankrupt spirituality of Protestantism is to be saved. But this would mean recognizing that another faith can be a teacher of spiritual things, and this is hard to accept. Some missionaries, taking a saving message to a poor dark people, have yet come to find that they had something to learn. They came to teach, they stayed to learn. But the process has often been agonizing and humiliating, as ingrained prejudices have been worn down.

But what can be learnt from other faiths? This question is often asked, partly through a feeling that we have all the answers, and partly because those who say we should learn from others are often very vague except in suggesting a wholesale transfer of eastern ideas. There are many points that might be suggested, and we must be content with but a few examples. An Indian missionary being asked this question, 'Give us one instance of what we can learn from Hinduism', replied, 'The love of God for his own sake, and not for anything he gives'. And one of the greatest of Chinese missionaries, replying to a similar challenge, answered from his profound knowledge of Buddhism, 'A sense of the immensities of space and time that are at God's disposal for his work, so that we are delivered from the so-much-to-do-so-little-done anxiety of the West.'[6]

Others have pointed the contrast between the two great imperial patrons of world religions, Ashoka and Constantine. Constantine's profession of Christianity was not wholly due to political craft, but undoubtedly it helped the unification of the empire and he gradually forbade heathen sacrifices; cruel acts after his 'conversion', such as the execution of his eldest son and his second wife, marred his reign even

[6] E. L. Allen, *op. cit.*, p. 153.

though he was not baptized till his death-bed. But the legend of his vision of the cross in battle, 'in this sign conquer', was a presage of the association of the church with the state and with persecution that was soon to take place. Ashoka, on the other hand, in the third century B.C., was filled with remorse at the sight of the misery caused by war. No doubt his conquests were exaggerated by later legends, but clearly he became a man of peace and an ardent disciple of the Buddha. In the edicts which he had carved on rocks and pillars, many of which still remain, he speaks of his sorrow at the unhappiness caused to victims of warfare. 'If a hundredth or a thousandth part of these were now to suffer the same fate, it would be a matter of deep sorrow to his majesty. Though one should do him an injury, his majesty now holds that it must be patiently borne.' His good works, hospitals, rest-houses, prohibition of hunting, and care for animals, as well as his propagation of Buddhism but tolerance of other teachings, made him one of the greatest rulers of mankind; H. G. Wells called Ashoka one of the six greatest men of history.

Many Christians have been gentle, patient, tolerant, and suffering, and true followers of Christ himself. But others have not, and it is partly the pride of these that makes them demand what they can possibly learn from other religions. They need to take to heart the charge that the claim to possess absolute truth is largely responsible for the national fanaticisms of today. Not only in politics but in religion the sense of being always right easily brings aggressiveness. Rabindranath Tagore once said to an inquirer, 'Your Western mind is too much obsessed with the idea of conquest and possession; your inveterate habit of proselytism is another form of it . . . Preaching your doctrine is no sacrifice at all—it is indulging in a luxury far more dangerous than all the luxuries of material living. It breeds an illusion in your mind that you are doing your duty—that you are wiser and better than your fellow-beings. But the real preaching is in being perfect, which is through meekness and love and self-dedication.'[7]

If one can have the patience and humility to learn from

[7] in *Mahatma Gandhi's Ideas*, a letter quoted by C. F. Andrews, p. 356.

others and from their teachings and truths, then new light may be brought upon one's own faith. This religion of ours, which is what we have made of it in the West, may be enriched and illuminated from other traditions. Some of the best missionaries have recognized this. 'Individual soul (*Jivatma*) and Supreme Soul or Over-Soul (*Paramatma*)—who are they, and what is the relation between them? A doctrine which makes God a merely transcendental Being—the Creator of man and wholly separate from him—and man a finite and subordinate creature, utterly distinct from God, cannot be final, it is not the whole truth and it does not satisfy. "I and the Father are one", "That they may be one as we are one"—what is the meaning of these phrases? They recognize the mystery of our being, of the relation of us men to God; and they contain a profound suggestion of fellowship and unity in God of which we have but dimly conceived, which we express still less perfectly.'[8]

[8] E. W. Thompson, *The Word of the Cross to Hindus*, p. 63.

CHAPTER 8

COMPLEMENTARY RELIGIONS

I belong to the church of which I am a member because I was born into it. That is a plain statement of fact, and it applies to many other people. Its implications are far-reaching. Of course there are many other reasons which I now adduce for belonging to my church. I have a clear idea of what its teachings are, and I think they conform to the ancient and orthodox doctrines of the universal church. I have come to love its wisdom and its patterns of worship. I have also learnt to appreciate some of the ways of other churches, but with all their claims to catholicity I have not felt impelled to leave my own fold and join theirs. I feel the wisdom of Von Hügel's advice to Evelyn Underhill, that one should not leave one's own church unless convinced that it is a sin to stay in it. No church is perfect, as no religion is absolute, and it is better to learn from other churches and gradually grow together than to cause continual breaches by changing from one to another.

In the ecumenical movement many of the old misunderstandings have been removed and a new spirit of charity has appeared in the last fifty years. We have learnt a great deal from each other and have drawn much closer together. Yet the differences which separate us have grown sharper, in some respects, for we see more clearly what each has been standing for. If corporate union is to be accomplished it will take a long time yet. And if it does come about between the larger and older churches, there are still many small groups which remain separate. Still more ominously there are vigorous minorities today which in some measure replace the dissenters of yesterday. Pentecostalists function now in some way as Methodists did in the last century, and Christian Scientists as the old faith-healers. There are differences of temperament and expression which arise out of basic human needs.

C. G. Jung was an extreme left wing Protestant, yet he asserts, 'I am firmly convinced that a vast number of people belong to the fold of the Catholic Church and nowhere else, because they are most suitably housed there.' Their religion is of the intuitive and unquestioning kind, and that explains the growth of catholicism in this country where it meets the needs of many people. But there is also the accident of birth to consider, and those who accept religion without question would remain Presbyterian in Scotland, Roman Catholic in Spain, and Orthodox in Greece. Perhaps the majority of people are like this, and even those of us who question some things prefer not to make a great change.

But Jung continues with a claim for religious liberty. 'I believe, too, that there must be protestants against the Catholic Church, and also protestants against Protestantism —for the manifestations of the spirit are truly wondrous, and as varied as Creation itself.'[1] There are those who are born to be Luthers and village Hampdens. A religion that is truly catholic would no doubt make room for turbulent as well as for submissive souls, but, especially in the West, the temptations of authority and power have brought restriction and repression.

If I had been born in Burma I should almost certainly be a Buddhist today, and in Japan a Shintoist. That is a sobering thought, which fundamentalist advocates of the view that all non-Christians are damned seem hardly to have considered. Still less do they appear to have thought what reflection upon the character of God is implied in this sweeping view. That very few Burmese Buddhists have become Christians seems to suggest also that those of Protestant nature find sufficient scope in that religion. Or at least Christianity has not been presented to them in a sufficiently attractive or intelligible a manner as to persuade them to adopt it.

Is it possible between the religions to regard one as complementary to another, presenting teachings lacking in the other which may be taken over at will? It is all very well to regard churches, in what is on the whole the same religion, as offering different aspects of the faith to varying individuals, and borrowing rites and practices from each other because the accompanying doctrines are not wholly incom-

1 *Modern Man in Search of a Soul*, p. 282.

patible with the main body of faith. But can this be done at all with different systems of belief? Will it not lead to a syncretistic religion which is artificial and lacking in conviction?

Yet the claim that religions can be complementary to one another has been made by several writers recently, and most notably by Toynbee. In *An Historian's Approach to Religion* he says that 'the missions of the higher religions are not competitive; they are complementary'. And the same point was developed in his *Study of History*, where he took the psychological approach. Beginning with the notion of compensation, he said that over-development in one direction injures the personality and brings about reaction. A religion that stresses one aspect of the truth provokes a counter-action. So if Roman Catholicism allows Christ to be obscured by the Virgin Mary there arises a Protestant reaction. But this in turn excludes the feminine element in religion and Anglo-Catholicism appears to supply it. In India the *advaita* teaching appears to dissolve belief in a personal God, and Buddhism to dismiss God altogether, and the *bhakti* cults develop to provide for this deep religious requirement and are followed by the Amidist forms of Mahāyāna Buddhism.

Between the religions perhaps the same might apply, each of them existing to supply some element lacking in the other. This would explain the diversity of the world's religions. It would also show that none possesses the final truth, and their history shows that they do not meet all human needs. Toynbee develops this thesis by invoking Jung's classification of psychological types. The extrovert religions are Christianity, Judaism and Islam, because they worship a transcendent creator God, who is above and beyond man. The introvert religions are Hinduism and Buddhism, because they seek the divine within and stress feeling or intuition. So, says Toynbee, 'the divers higher religions must resign themselves to playing limited parts, and must school themselves to playing these parts in harmony, in order, between them, to fulfil their common purpose of enabling every human being or every psychological type to enter into communion with God the Ultimate Reality'.[2]

But generalizations can be misleading. It must not be supposed that all Asian peoples are introverted and all Europeans extroverts; our history can give plenty examples of both. Moreover each religion contains divisions and sects that cater for different types, intellectual and intuitive, and if they had not done so they would hardly have retained their sway over so many people for so long.

The differences of religions are traditional and would need a great deal of study to explain adequately. It is more important to seek affinities between them. And in this the complexity of religions can be a valuable ally. It has often been remarked that various types of Christianity resemble certain types of other religions. When the Jesuit missionaries to Japan found the Buddhist sects teaching salvation by faith alone in Amida they cried out 'this is Lutheranism'. The ritual and organization of Tibetan Lamaism has often been compared with Roman Catholicism. And Sunni Islam has been likened to Unitarianism. There are patterns of religious experience in one religion that appeal to like forms in another. As Allen says, 'The religions are like cities, each of which has within it a group of people related by kinship to the people of other cities. While they retain their loyalty unimpaired, they can therefore interpret to their rulers the policies of those other cities and so make friendship possible where otherwise hostility would threaten.'[3]

The fascination which some other religions, particularly Hinduism and Buddhism, have for western man is partly due to the feeling of kinship which many experience for them. Sometimes they may indicate something lacking in our own religious tradition, more often they express themselves in a gentler and more attractive way. The Hindu conception of God may suggest more reverence, by its very negatives, than the dogmatic and sometimes crude language of the West. Buddhist teachings and practices show that fervour can be persuasive rather than harshly authoritarian. Both these religions have a vista of long ages for the perfection of the soul, which are more generous than the speedy but

[2] *A Study of History*, vii, p. 734.
[3] *Christianity among the Religions*, p. 142.

then lasting hell-fire promised in Semitism after a short span on earth. And at the mystical level there are depths of devotion that have a universal appeal.

Toynbee, however, is concerned not simply to press for recognition of the complementary aspects of religion, but to urge the need for religions to join forces in face of the fearful adversary that confronts them all, and he develops this in later books.

In days gone by if a Christian were asked what was the greatest enemy of his faith, he might well have replied Islam, or in India Hinduism and in China Buddhism. But today there is a much more dangerous rival, and he would be much more likely to reply Communism in all those countries. 'In our day Christianity and all the other living higher religions find themselves confronted by a common adversary, the old religion of man-worship in the form of the worship of collective human power.' This cult of power, which Communism and Fascism express, armed with the might of modern technology and fired by cruel fanaticism, strikes at the root of all spiritual religion. 'It challenges that enormously important negative article of faith that is common to all the higher religions: the conviction that Man is not the greatest spiritual presence in the Universe, but that there is a greater presence—God or absolute reality—and that the true end of Man is to place himself in harmony with this.'[4]

Toynbee holds that there is this common element at least between all religions, that they believe in spiritual reality, as distinct from the materialism of the bastard-religion Communism. He stresses the urgency of the recognition of this fact by religions, so that they lay aside their traditional rivalry and side with one another to preserve the highest cultural values of mankind and face the worst foe that has ever appeared against them. Squabbles between religions are like quarrels of mice when the cat is ready to spring on them all. Common action of religions need not mean at all that convictions should be abandoned. But it does demand laying aside old prejudices, as has already happened between the

[4] *Christianity among the Religions of the World*, p. 81.

churches, and that wherever we can work together we must do so.

There must be no under-estimate of the strength and determination of the anti-religious forces today, which are resolved to root out all religion. The Communist half of the world is pledged to atheism, and regards all religion as superstitious and feudalistic, 'the opiate of the masses' and the reason for their depressed state. In Russia the bitterest persecutions of the Church marked the early years of the revolution and have continued sporadically ever since; at the funeral of Boris Pasternak, a devout Christian, in 1960, not a word of Christian text or prayer was allowed to be uttered. No doubt the Russian Orthodox church was corrupt and subservient to the state, and reformation was overdue, but it was the only form of religion available to the great masses of the people, and still it attracts many people. In 1960 the Soviet Academy of Sciences made a study of the beliefs of the collective farmers and were shocked to find the hold that religion has upon them, with an increase in religious weddings and baptisms. After forty years this great dictatorship is still nervous of religion, and dare not allow free expression of opinion in writing: no English newspapers except the *Daily Worker* may be imported into Russia.

The same applies to China and Tibet. And here part of the attack on the traditional religion was led by the Christian missions. It was easy to denounce the idolatry of the Chinese village cults, with their red-faced war gods, city tutelary deities, and frightening pictures of many hells. As long ago as 1890 observers remarked on the carelessness with which images would be thrown out and used to fill up holes in the roads. Many missions were only shedding crocodile tears later when they deplored the Communist attack on all forms of religion, and there were comparatively few who had sought to enter into spiritual conversation with Confucians. Taoists or Buddhists. Had they done so they might have found that Confucian scholars have for centuries opposed the use of images in the cult of the 'teacher of a thousand generations', and that tablets had replaced idols in his shrines. Buddhist revival had begun, led by many of the laity, and was seeking to show the religion as a way of life for workers as well as monks. Taoists were the most corrupt, yet many of the powerful societies, such as the Pervading-Unity Tao, were theirs, and the Tao Tê Ching had been translated by Christian scholars and hailed as one of the world's great masterpieces. Tibetan lamaism has often been described as corrupt and a complete distortion of the original Buddhism if compared with the Theravāda Buddhism of Burma and Ceylon. But Buddhist scholars in recent years have questioned the character, and certainly our knowledge, of this 'original Buddhism'. It was the Protestant and agnostic British administrators of Ceylon and Burma who hailed the form of Buddhism found there as original, and thought they had found a religion of pure rationalism, without miracle, God, soul, or 'numinous' object of worship. A reading of any of the Jātaka tales of the Buddha, as popular in Ceylon as in China, ought to have dispelled some of these illusions. In any case, Buddhism is the dominant religion of Tibet, and however soon or late the Dalai Lama returns from his exile Buddhism will be the faith of Tibet for long yet, unless the whole population is deported to China. The International Commission of Jurists has proved beyond doubt that the Chinese have tried to stamp out Buddhism from Tibet completely, by destroying monasteries and temples and killing or enslaving the monks.

But if the Christian missions were not sorry to witness the destruction of some old and superstitious forms of religion, and some better ones, they themselves were to come under attack in due course. The wheel turned full circle. Christianity also was superstitious and, worse, it was foreign and imperialistic. Even before the Communist victory in China many young people were anti-religious and attacked Christianity as an enemy to progress. Tang Liang Li in his book *China in Revolt* wrote: 'Young China is determined to put an end to the attempt of the Christian missions to dominate China's spiritual life. For they are convinced that Christianity in its decay has nothing to offer thoughtful people—clergy or lay—even in the West; since it is morally defective, intellectually absurd and historically untrue, it is not a suitable religion for the awakening Chinese who are certainly not a nation of savages! The enlightened West still believes in Joshua miraculously changing the sun in its course, and in the Immaculate Conception. Young China, on the contrary, is no longer prepared to be nourished by an inferior philosophy, by impracticable ethics, by the foolish superstitions and myths of the old world which are passed off by the majority of missionaries in China as divine revelation and historical truth.'[5]

Of course the Chinese will retort that there is freedom of religion, that since the revolution there have been established Chinese Buddhist, Taoist and Islamic Associations, under governmental patronage. The clue is in the last words, for they are completely under official control and subservient to every decree of authority. Countless temples, monasteries and Confucian halls have been sacked or taken over by the military, and their monks told to work. All Christian missionaries were expelled from China, and Protestant churches were forcibly united; in 1959 it was reliably reported that of 65 church buildings in Peking only 4 remained in use, and of Shanghai's 200 churches only 23 were still open. Rituals were unified by order and certain teachings prohibited.

The attack on religion is most vicious in the Communist countries, but it is insidious elsewhere in the growing materialism of other lands. Those who are deeply concerned for spiritual things, and who believe that religion expresses man's deepest need and profoundest apprehensions of this universe, must ask themselves which is worse, atheism or religion? There are some Christians who find it hard to accept Roman Catholicism, or the Salvation Army, as preferable to atheism. Many others have not asked themselves whether Islam is not better than atheism. Yet the Muslim, in his charity, regards Christianity as a spiritual way of life; and the Hindu and Buddhist believe that there are many ways to the truth. 'All God's names are hallowed.'

The same concern with the materialistic challenge to all forms of religion is expressed by Philip Ashby in *The Conflict of Religions*. For too long religions have thought of themselves as being in opposition to one another and have inherited past differences unthinkingly. Now in the grim

[5] Quoted in Ohm, *op. cit.*, p. 4.

situation of today they must adjust their ideas. 'Faced by enemies who would destroy them, they are also in conflict among themselves. Religion is the opponent of religion.' This way lies self-destruction, which atheist enemies will assist with pleasure. The house is not only divided against itself and in danger of destruction from within, but foes outside are helping on the process by knocking down the walls. Yet in this struggle against materialism there could be unexpected allies. Too long have Christians thought of themselves as fighting a lone battle against atheism, even a Protestant or fundamentalist battle. The effect of materialism upon other religions has hardly been noted and their struggle unobserved as if it were no concern of ours, or even the victory of atheism an ally. But religions together can find great new strength. 'Man has at his disposal a powerful and as yet relatively untried resource whereby he can meet the troubles of this age with confidence . . . This resource is the combined witness of the major religions of the world.'[6]

If the religions can side with each other, instead of trying to destroy each other, then their combined forces, appeal and insight, should provide sufficient armoury to pierce the indifference and antagonism of modern man to the claims of religion. Different religions, says Ashby, need not be equated with one another. In fact each has faced the problems of life from a different angle, and therefore each has an important contribution to make to modern needs and to the battle with atheism. By working together religions need not minimize their differences, but they can turn them to advantage by using their perceptions in a common cause.

Radhakrishnan made similar appeals long ago, but his pleas went largely unheeded, because the grim nature of the modern challenge to all religion was not so clear then as it has since become. But he deplored the manner in which religions combat one another, when a far worse foe is at the door. 'If the great religions continue to waste their energies in a fratricidal war instead of looking upon themselves as friendly partners in the supreme task of nourishing the spiritual life of mankind, the swift advance of secular humanism and moral materialism is assured.' So he urges

[6] pp. viif, 3.

a firm common front by the religions to meet the needs of men and the attacks of atheism. 'We cannot afford to waver in our determination that the whole of humanity shall remain a united people, where Muslim and Christian, Buddhist and Hindu shall stand together bound by common devotion.'[7]

Where there are great religions established, as distinct from disintegrating animism, the revival of those religions is the surest protection against Communism. The way to combat atheism in Muslim lands is not to weaken Islam, but to purge it from superstition and corruption. The example of the Anglican Church in Egypt and Ethiopia may be relevant. For there it has not sought to replace the decadent Coptic Church, but so to help it towards reform from within that the common Christian cause may be strengthened. Christianity is very weak in Arab countries, and cannot defeat Communism alone, but it may assist Islam to do so.

So it follows that a Christian should take no pleasure in the corruption of another religion, but should wish to see it at its finest and best. Human nature being frail it is all too easy for missionaries to seize on the weaknesses of another religion as a means of entry into its stronghold; and when speaking about it at home too often they depict the bad side as if it were the essence of the religion; this may be good propaganda but bad truth. Of course it is harder to plead one's own cause in face of the best of another religion. But if his own is indeed superior this can only be proved at the highest and not the lowest level. Christianity too can be criticized severely from its corruptions, but its supporters would maintain that such criticism was unfair, that it had 'never been tried'. Between religions, as between religions, we have said that the maxim must apply, 'As you would that men should do to you, do so also to them'.

Mahatma Gandhi, speaking to missionaries who had asked his advice about their work, said that they should seek to help and serve the people by making them better within their own traditions. 'Let them appear before the people as they are, and try to rejoice in seeing Hindus be-

[7] *Eastern Religions and Western Thought* (1939), p. 347.

come better Hindus, and Mussalmans better Mussalmans.'[8]

It may well be asked whether this is consistent with one's own religious belief. But it can be if truth is admitted in other religions, and if their role is regarded as complementary. So at least Toynbee claims, 'The missions of the higher religions are not competitive; they are complementary. We can believe in our own religion without having to feel that it is the sole repository of truth. We can love it without having to feel that it is the sole means of salvation.'[9]

Christianity and Islam have been great missionary religions, and that they will continue to be so is realized by many Hindus. But the manner in which they exercise their function is of the utmost importance. Buddhism has evangelized half Asia, by peaceful persuasion, and Hinduism itself is stirring with missionary activity. But there is a great difference between evangelism, telling of the good news, and proselytism, seeking to win others into one particular fold. It is this latter imperialism and intolerance that has been condemned, and in some of the highest missionary circles. The International Missionary Council at Jerusalem in 1928 declared, 'We would repudiate any symptoms of a religious imperialism that would desire to impose beliefs and practices on others in order to manage their souls in their supposed interests. We obey a God who respects our wills and we desire to respect those of others.' The next council at Tambaram in 1938 suffered the attacks of Kraemer and the Barthian reaction against all that it regarded as liberalism. But the further reaction to a more tolerant attitude is now demanded in face of the militant atheism of our times.

The ideal relationship between religions is that in which they support all that is good in each other's faith and unite against all that is bad. The aim of dialogue between faiths is not just proselytism, winning souls as so many scalps, and laying up merit for oneself in heaven. So a Christian theologian says, 'The Christian can enter into conversation with men and women of another faith because his aim in this is not to win them for his religion, but to serve that kingdom of Christ whose triumphs are only those of truth and love.'

[8] *Mahatma Gandhi's Ideas*, p. 357.
[9] *An Historian's Approach to Religion*, p. 296f.

The light of Christ can be shown, without insisting that those who accept it should swell some particular denomination and increase its statistics. 'He does not demand that all become Christians. For he knows that Christendom has so sadly misinterpreted Christ that he may draw some to himself within their own religions as he could do by gaining them for ours.'[10]

The service of religion today is to preserve freedom for man. This is greatly threatened, by all manner of states, which force men into servitude with the claim that it is all for his material advantage and eventual comfort. The protest of Aldous Huxley's savage is relevant here: 'I don't want comfort—I want God, I want poetry, I want real danger, I want freedom, I want goodness, I want sin.'[11] In this battle for the soul of man all allies are welcome, and above all our fellow men of religion, of all faiths. In Wesley's words, we should be 'friends of all and enemies of none.' We do not need to demand conformity of doctrine, but in true catholic spirit should ask, 'Is thy heart right, if so, give me thy hand.'

[10] E. L. Allen, *Christianity among the Religions*, p. 155.
[11] *Brave New World*, p. 283.

CHAPTER 9

REVIVAL AND CRITICISM

A religion seen from within is very different from what it looks like from the outside, which is why it is so important to listen to men of other faiths expressing what their religion means to them. The outside observer can hardly help comparing the other religion with his own, which he knows from the inside, and judging the externals unfavourably. So it is that in the past a great deal of criticism has been expressed of Asian religions, by judging them on externals. Practices that surprised or shocked Europeans were denounced, and all the religion with them, without much effort to discover the meaning of the customs and whether they were truly typical or degenerations. Much early, and still some later, missionary propaganda centred on the aberrations rather than the essence of the religion.

Such an approach is dangerous, not only because it so easily lends itself to injustice, but also because it is liable to be turned round and directed against the foreign religion that sets itself up as judge. So Allen remarks, 'Most of our criticisms of a religion other than our own are invalid for the simple reason that it is one thing for those who live by it and another for those who do not. We turn aside attacks on Christianity by pleading that they are valid only against "empirical", not against "genuine" Christianity. But what is to prevent a Buddhist from urging that Buddhism has not failed, it has been found difficult and not tried?'[1]

Not only so but many of the criticisms that have been made of Asian religions are either out of date or rapidly becoming so. The word Juggernaut has entered into the English language, although the temple of Jagannātha (a title of the god Krishna) at Puri has long since ceased to witness the spectacle of ecstatic devotees dragging the divine car with hooks in their backs, or throwing themselves under its wheels. Suttee (*sati*), widow-burning, has been forbidden for a century and it was a limited and degenerate practice even

1 *Christianity among the Religions*, p. 145

in its heyday. Discrimination against castes has not fully disappeared, nor has colour-distinction in some Christian countries, yet it has been made illegal by the independent Indian republic and its leaders fight against it. But all these and other practices may be cited as evidences of the nature of Hinduism, despite the fact that none of them is essential to the religion.

Further, the revival and resurgence of Hinduism is an undoubted fact, and if there are still masses that are ignorant of the reforms advocated by their leaders, the same might be said of reformations in other countries. That Hinduism was in a decline in the last century is undoubted, and of other religions too it may be said that they suffered varying degrees of stagnation, and that the advent of Western culture has served to revive and reform them. The Reformation and Renaissance that Europe had known in the sixteenth century only came to other religions in the nineteenth.

But in Hinduism the foundation of the Brāhmo Samāj, by Rām Mohan Roy, took place as long ago as 1828 and was the precursor of a long series of revival movements. Rām Mohan himself opposed polytheism and idolatry, polygamy and suttee and took a leading part in the abolition of the latter practice. The Brāhmo Samāj was monotheistic and friendly towards other religions, such as Islam and Christianity. The later Arya Samāj was more militantly Hindu, and the Hindu Mahāsabhā and the Rāshtriya Sevak Sangh have sought to make Hinduism the state religion, though so far unsuccessfully, and as a secular state India guarantees freedom to all religions.

There is little doubt that the pressures of modern times have brought a resurgence of Hinduism and a self-awareness that is a new feature. The religious struggles with Islam, the formation of Pakistan, the riots and massacres at the time of partition in 1947, have all helped to consolidate Hinduism. They have fostered the sense of communalism, with all its possibilities for good and evil.

How far the Hindu resurgence is truly religious has been questioned. There is no doubt that political motives have been very powerful, and it does not appear that temples are more frequented than in the past, though some of the great festivals, such as the Kumbha Melas are attended by vast crowds brought by modern means of transport, and religious teachers use megaphones and broadcasting to spread their messages on such occasions. Devanandan has pointed out that unlike the Buddhist monks of Ceylon and Burma, the Brahmin priests and non-Brahmin sacrificers do not act as popular religious leaders, indeed they are often opposed because of their social domination. Significantly many of the reforms have been begun by 'laymen', such as the Tagores and Gandhi. Yet in this is their strength, they are not bound to a priestly class, can welcome fresh ideas, and show the abiding appeal of Hinduism to the ordinary mind. Nobody can read the autobiographies of Gandhi or Devendranath Tagore without being impressed by the effect of Hindu teaching upon modern men.

New efforts that are being made to express Hinduism in modern terms, make its teachings more widely available, and offer itself as inclusive of all that is best in religion, are factors of our time that must be taken into account. Early missionaries had great difficulty in finding out what Hinduism really taught, and they complained of the 'distant hauteur' of the Brahmins, their scorn of strangers and especially of Europeans, 'the jealous inquietude with which they hide from the profane the mysteries of their religious cult; the records of their learning; the privacy of their homes; all these form barriers between themselves and their observers which it is almost impossible to pass.' That was in 1897, how different from 1957 when a young French woman could write of the way in which she shared the life of a Brahmin home as a member of the family.[2]

Hinduism is often set out today as *sanātana dharma*, eternal religion, whose origins are lost in the mists of antiquity but go back to the ancient rishis and to the divine who revealed the Vedas. It is also eternal in that it has a boundless future, it can take up and adapt all new aspects of truth, for it is inclusive. Hence all forms of Indian re-

[2] J. A. Dubois and H. K. Beauchamp, *Hindu Manners, Customs* and *Ceremonies*, p. 12; and L. Reymond, *My Life with a Brahmin Family*.

ligion, from primitive cults to advanced philosophy can find a place in its ample embrace.

The point that we are trying to make is that these modern forms of religion are the ones with which we have to deal today, and not with old abuses or closed in systems. Those who speak to other religions are followers of one of the Samājs, or Vinoba Bhave's Sarvadaya, believing that all religions are equal, or perhaps followers of the theosophical movement which, often neglected in study, has yet been very potent in the revival of Hinduism and recognition of truths in other religions. Similarly the Rāmakrishna Mission and Neo-Vedāntic movements are the representatives in the West of the most active forms of Hinduism. To these, then, and to a purified and reviving Hinduism must attention be drawn, and not to the abuses of the old and unreformed cults.

Similarly in Islam there has been such reaction and revolution that a new situation must be recognized. Islamic reaction to modern times has taken two main forms, first there is the Puritan reform of the Wahhābi of Arabia, who control the sacred shrines, try to expunge corrupt practices like saint-worship, and return to primitive forms of Islam. There is no doubt of their fervour and piety, and a similar reaction may be seen among the Senussi of Cyrenaica. On the other hand are the reforming movements, particularly strong in Egypt and Pakistan, where many of the leaders have been educated in western schools and universities. Perhaps their greatest representative was Sir Mohammad Ipbāl, whose *Reconstruction of Religious Thought in Islam* is still significant. In Turkey the revolution went the furthest and rejection of many old customs, and the authority of traditional Islamic law, was most sweeping. Yet the Turks claim not to have renounced Islam but to have got rid of priestcraft, and to be true Muslims by re-stating the religion in modern terms. They have achieved quickly and violently what is being done slowly but surely elsewhere in the Muslim world, and the Turks regard themselves as leaders for the Arab people to follow, as they have done for centuries.

These reformations have also produced offshoots in sects,

such as the Ahmadiyya which claim Ghulām Ahmad (died 1908) as Messiah and Mahdi and teach a number of variant doctrines from the orthodox. The Bahā'ī movement also, found in Europe and America as well as the East, began as a revival but moved outside Islam to become a universal religion, with the Bāb as the latest prophet. Those religions that claim they are best because latest, always run the risk of being counter-challenged by a new prophet. But these movements are now outside the main Islamic revival, and conversations with Islam would not be fruitfully directed to them.

Criticisms of Islam have often picked on social customs, such as polygamy and the veil, that are not of the essence of the religion at all. *Punch* still prints cartoons of the predicaments of veiled ladies or their admirers, which get wearisome and are in the questionable taste of poking fun at other people's customs as the Victorian cartoonists did at the ignorance or bad grammar of the lower classes. But veiling, perhaps originally adopted from Syrian Christianity, has been abolished in Turkey for the last forty years and is rapidly going elsewhere; the nylon veils worn by young ladies in Pakistan are rather fetching and mere tributes to custom.

Polygamy is a more serious issue, but it was practised for reasons similar to those observed by many of the Old Testament saints. Muhammad had nine wives, desiring a male heir as earnestly as Henry VIII, sovereign of the English church and reformation, with his six wives. Although the Qur'ān permits a man, if he can 'act equitably', to take up to four legal wives, yet most Muslims today are monogamous and there are strong movements in favour of making this universal. In 1958 it was claimed that ninety-four per cent of Egyptian Muslims had only one wife and in 1959 Tunisia was the first Islamic state to make monogamy the only legal form of marriage. So strong is the pressure of public opinion in favour of reform.

It is the reformers who are concerned in the dialogue of religion today, and they are more concerned even than outside critics to see that the abuses of Islam are cleared away. It is the young scholars and writers of the new universities and cities that are interested in new approaches to the life of Jesus, or in translations of the Qur'ān. In 1954, as a result of a meeting at Bhandun, Lebanon, sponsored by the American Friends of the Middle East, a Continuing Committee was set up which has striven to further the aims of Muslim-Christian Co-operation.

In Buddhism too account must be taken of the modern forms in which the religion is presented in its contacts with the West. Quiescent for a time under colonial rule the resurgence of Buddhism has become clear in this century. In the 2,500 years of Buddhism only six general councils are recognized by the Theravāda (Hīnayāna) Buddhists of southern Asia. The fifth council was held in Burma in 1871, when the chief scriptures were inscribed on hundreds of marble slabs. The sixth Council, to celebrate the Buddha's Jāyanti, 'victory' of birth, enlightenment, and entry into Parinirvāna was held in Rangoon from 1954 to 1956. Here the scriptures were collated and prepared for translation into many western languages, and a great World Peace pagoda opened to show Buddhism as a religion of peace.

Reforms of Buddhist worship and doctrine are less clearly marked. In his *Revolt in the Temple,* D. C. Vijayavardhana of Ceylon criticizes not only the many Buddhas and Bodhisattvas of northern Mahāyāna Buddhism, but also the teaching of Buddhist monks in his own country. 'The Buddhism taught by some members of our Sangha is downright pessimism. They lay stress on the presence of suffering in the world to the exclusion of all else. Life, in their eyes, is a bleak and dismal procession to the grave. The Sangha, by parodying sorrow and suffering, is tying what are virtually millstones round the necks of the people.' So he suggests that a social religion, stressing the brotherhood of mankind and active love is the true Way of Virtue taught by the Buddha.

Both this writer and a number of Buddhist apologists in the West stress the rationality of Buddhism, and play down the supernatural element and legend as past or false to the religion. By its rationalism and also its following of nature Buddhism is presented as eminently a religion for men trained in the ways of modern science. This leads frequently to stress upon the atheistic element in Buddhism (or trans-theistic as Zimmer called it). Whether this really is inherent in Buddhism, and whether a religion can exist, or has survived, without a belief in some divine object, must be the subject of long and careful conversations with Buddhists. Certainly prominent and devout leaders like U Nu of Burma have recognized the danger of atheistic Communism to Buddhism, for he has spoken of 'the machinations of those who are out to destroy the very foundations of our religion. Their methods are very subtle and their intention is undoubtedly sinister. From certain quarters Lord Buddha's omniscience has been questioned and ridiculed. Worse than that some even go to the extent of declaring that Lord Buddha was a lesser man than Karl Marx'. And he concluded this speech to the Burmese parliament by saying that Buddhism had no aim of disparaging other spiritual religions, such as Christianity, Hinduism or Islam, but of fighting the anti-religious forces that are raising their ugly heads everywhere.

A strong influence in the revival of Buddhism is the need for social reform and political independence. Hence leaders such as U Nu were able not only to take their country into self-government but also to show that their driving power was a Buddhism that impelled all their actions. The new respect for religion, which has been described as being as strong as in Victorian England, is a feature of modern south-east Asian countries. As in the Middle East the struggle against Communism must be led by Islam, so it must be led by Buddhism in southern Asia; for in Burma there are only twelve thousand Christians, to twelve million Buddhists.

The stress on Buddhism as a religion of peace is particularly significant today. The way of the Buddha was always peaceful, and this religion has the best record of any for peaceful ways, though there have been some violent figures at times. But the dropping of the atomic bombs on Japan has focused attention on the role of Buddhism in bringing peace to the world. Some have called it the dropping of bombs by Christians on Buddhists, others have said that Christianity has failed to bring the peace that it claims to strive at. More positively Buddhism is set out as the way to peace, both for the individual life and for the affairs of nations.

In the confrontation of religions these new Buddhist leaders are the ones who must be met, their claims must be considered, and together ways must be worked out of living in the modern world.

Similar things might be said of other religions, of their changes and adaptations to modern conditions, but space forbids it here. But it must be recognized that the process of adaptation is going on, that reforms are being affected. Therefore it is necessary to study these modern forms, and take the religion at its face value. As Allen says, 'the religions of the East are not defunct, they are taking on new forms to meet the challenge of the modern world. We allow that such a procedure is legitimate in our own case, but seem to regard it as unfair when, say, Islam follows our example. We want to stereotype the other religions so that we can always feel superior to them. They ought to stagnate and die. But they refuse to oblige us. We must allow a religion to be what its followers claim that it is.'[3]

If other religions are judged by their failings then this standard can be turned against the West. Since this book will be read mainly, though it is to be hoped not exclusively, by Western Christians, it is perhaps desirable to make some reference here to the ways in which the East views the West and its religion.

It is a salutary, and often painful, experience to try to see ourselves as others see us. We have an image of ourselves which we project and expect others to share our viewpoint, which they cannot possibly do. Different facets of our character appear to them, which may counterbalance the good façade.

The West, believing in its own superiority, material and it thinks spiritual, takes up an attitude to the rest of the world which it may regard as charitable but others often see as arrogance. Dispensers of charity, builders of hospitals and schools, promoters of tribal peace and democracy, the West indeed has great achievements to its credit which no

[3] *op. cit.*, p. 145.

doubt later centuries will remember. But it is a common human trait to resent superior benefactors and liberators, and we cannot buy the affection of the East with money. And unhappily there are other sides of western culture which disfigure the good.

Somebody has said that Russia need spend no money on anti-American propaganda in Asia. Hollywood does it much better for her. For many of the films sent by Hollywood throughout Asia present a picture of American life that shocks Asian peoples. The vulgar luxury, the gross sensuality, the crude violence of many cheap American films present a picture that is repulsive. If this is the American way of life, Asians say, we do not want it. Is not America a Christian country, and Hollywood a Christian town, with many churches and ministers? Then let us retain our own culture and religion. So a moral judgement is passed, and the religion condemned along with the culture, as the West has often condemned Islam for polygamy or India for caste.

Omdurman is a town where most of the women still wear burqas, the veil that covers them from head to foot. But I remember seeing there advertisements for a film in which an American woman dressed in riding breeches stood with a whip in her hand over a prostrate man, and the shocked comments of Muslims on female emancipation were audible. Many British films are little better, and many Asian students in London have wandered unwittingly into a cinema showing an X film, and have been shocked at the parade of naked women and exploited violence.

Add to this the effect of nuclear weapons, that atomic bombs were dropped on distant and coloured people, and one can understand the shock, as Canon Raven put it, 'when the result of a generation of intense scientific effort was announced to the world in the name of the two Christian democracies by the annihilation of a city'. So the Japanese and eastern Buddhist world claims that Christianity has failed and that Buddhism is the only religion that can bring peace to the world.

Not only in Asia have moral judgements been passed on the West for its arrogant and barbaric ways. Even in Africa people have not been slow to perceive our failings. The

European is often regarded as proud, bad-tempered, gluttonous, sensual and inhospitable. There is no doubt of his pride, demonstrated in his treatment of lesser breeds and coloured races. His bad temper in a hot climate, in which no doubt subordinates provoke him, is an extension of his general irritability and lack of peace. He is gluttonous in eating four or five meals a day, several of them with meat, while those around him can rarely afford more than one or two. His sensuality is obvious in the large 'coloured' populations he creates; the 'Immorality Acts' of South Africa are products of a guilty conscience about the past and efforts to control the present. Perhaps worst of all, in both African and Asian eyes, the Westerner is inhospitable, for hospitality is a cardinal virtue in the East. But if one visits a European at his home he may well not ask you inside, if inside you may not be offered a seat, or if that then not a drink, and almost certainly a coloured person will not be invited to take a meal at table, and hardly ever is he asked to spend the night even if he is far from home.

The superiority of a white skin is not obvious to everybody. The Bishop of Uganda used to tell how an old man explained his first impressions of Europeans. Only with much reluctance did he speak, but after much pressing he admitted, 'When I first saw a European woman, I went behind a banana tree and was sick.' White skin, no doubt with Victorian clothing, was no mark of beauty or superiority. The colour bar may work both ways. White people are in a minority, in the Commonwealth and in the world. The Aryan pride of colour which produced the word caste (*varna*), turns back upon itself.

Not only are the morals of the West judged and found wanting, but its religion as well. An obvious weakness is the disunity of Christianity and this is exported to the East. 'There is scarcely a territory or even a larger township in Asia without its missions of various Christian denominations, all fighting against each other. The consequences are evident. It is impossible, Asians will say, that a religion with so many different doctrines, customs, orders, and organizations can be the true faith. In any case, it would be difficult to discover the right denomination. If even Europeans cannot find their way about, how can Asians be expected to discover theirs?'[4] National and denominational differences have been exported in an absurd fashion. There was a Dutch Reformed Church of Canada in China. And since the Second World War there have been established fifty-nine different Christian sects in Formosa, whereas before the war there was only one. Can it be wondered that these are regarded as foreign and divisive? The restrictions placed by some eastern governments on missions are aimed particularly at these tiny sects, many of them American, which have flooded Formosa, Japan, and everywhere that was open in the East.

Complaints against the disunity of Christianity are not made simply on political or social grounds, but on religious grounds. Outstanding converts, like Sadhu Sundar Singh and Toyohiko Kagawa, preferred to remain outside organized religion. The former refused ordination in the Anglican church when he found he would be unable to preach in any other church, and he wrote, 'sects are strange and superfluous things. There is only one God—why, then, are there so many churches?' He saw in the confessional churches a 'relic of the caste system at the heart of Christianity'.

For others Christianity has betrayed Christ and exports only an inferior brand of religion. According to Rabindranath Tagore the West never really understood Christianity, and Gandhi refused to believe that if Christ appeared in the West he would recognize the churches, their liturgy and clergy. Lin Yutang objected to the conformity of the Churches with the state and held that they had never learnt to follow Christ whatever the consequences. Uchimura in Japan objected to the dogmatism and clerical control of the churches. While Sundar Singh found that the greatest lack of the West was the peace of God, like many other Asians he was shocked that Christians never meditate.

These are religious criticisms, and quite apart from attacks on dogma which might be launched by members of another religion. Most critics, however, make a clear distinction between Christianity and Christ; it is the religion as it has been fashioned in the West that comes under such

[4] Ohm, *Asia looks at Western Christianity*, p. 9.

heavy attack. The New Testament is known and treasured in many Asian countries. The Gospels are probably quoted more often in the newspapers in India and Japan than they are in England. Perhaps that is not very difficult, but great reverence is accorded to Jesus as teacher of love and peace. The Brāhmo Samāj and many Indian leaders have spoken of Christ in the highest terms. Buddhists have written of him as the personification of the truth (dharmakāya). Muslims respect the Gospels, and revere Jesus and Mary.

So that a distinction is made between what we ourselves might claim as 'genuine' Christianity, and 'empirical' western religion. The Gospels and Christ have made a profound impact on Asia in modern times. But 'the position of European Christianity is entirely different. The overwhelming majority have little sympathy for it. It has, we are told, little or nothing to do with Christ. In the opinion of many Asians, Europe has long lost all real understanding of Christ and his teaching; the essence of Christianity has been watered down. It is not taken seriously; Europe no longer accepts the radicalism of the Bible; it completely lacks the revolutionary fervour of genuine Christianity. Over and over again Asians will repeat: Europe has betrayed Christianity, its most sacred possession.'[5]

These things have been written not in an attempt to shock, or exaggerate, or underestimate the good that has been done. But so as to listen to what others do say about us, and to induce more care and charity when we speak about them. If we demand that 'true' Christianity must be studied so they demand that 'true' Buddhism, Islam or Hinduism be our object.

If there is to be any judgement or comparison of religions it must be by their best, and not by their worst. With what measure we judge, we shall be judged. And if we recognize that other religions stand in need of reform, this cannot be done in a spirit of superiority as if we needed no reform in our own religion. We need it as much as they do. We can learn from other religions, and from the religious and moral criticisms they offer to us. We can learn from their criticism

[5] *ibid.*, p. 13.

to seek the essence of our own faith better. We can learn from their religion.

Cantwell Smith has suggested the application of the parable of the Good Samaritan to the relationships of the religions today. The Jews, after the time of Nehemiah and Ezra, were filled with a sense of their religious superiority, excluded the Samaritans from their covenant and had destroyed their temple. In the parable Jesus showed not merely a neighbour, but an enemy and member of another religion, showing pity where the priest and levite, clerics of the orthodox religion, had failed. In modern terms we might see the Muslim or Buddhist showing us by their charity how to fulfil the duty that our own religion had commanded us.

CHAPTER 10

TASKS OF COMPARATIVE RELIGION

In the foregoing pages attempts have been made to face some of the problems which the comparative study of religions poses. There are attitudes of pride and prejudice, which must give way before the new situation of our times. Now some suggestions will be made as to what comparative religion should seek to do.

The first thing is to insist that religions matter, that their study is important, and that universities and governments should take them seriously.

Professor Cantwell Smith has said that a hundred years ago the standard western approach to Asia was that its religions were wrong. 'More recently the standard secular attitude has been that its religions do not matter—that progress consists in leaving behind "the shackles of the past" and substituting valves for values.'[1] In the projects and aid given to and in the East attention is naturally directed towards material conditions. But that is no reason for the total disregard of the religions of Asia as if they were factors of no importance.

Some encouragement to the secular attitude has been given by the Communist success in China and the manner in which it has swept away so much of the ancient religion and idolatry. But not only are there officially recognized Buddhist, Taoist and Islamic associations in China today, and restoration of great religious monuments and monasteries, but also there is evidence that even some of the young are reading the Confucian classics. It is too soon to judge, but it is difficult to imagine that China with its great national pride will forever reject its own great Confucian and Taoist writings. Of Tibet it can confidently be predicted that Buddhism will remain deeply enrooted in the lives of the people, as long as they live there.

The close association of religion with national movements in India and south Asian countries has been sufficiently

[1] *The Christian and the Religions of Asia*, p. 5.

stressed, certainly it would be as foolish to neglect the influence of religion among the Hindus or Burmese as it would among the Jews. And in the Arab world so many of the misunderstandings that have marred our relationships have arisen from our unwillingness or blindness in realizing that Arabs are Muslims and are shaped by the consciousness of a great and successful religious past.

A sign of the disregard for religion in dealings with the East is the almost complete lack of interest in the Asian classics. This is 'every whit as arrogant as the dogmatic religious one, and a good deal more helpless'. Yet this is at the same time as the common man has available such floods of material about other religions, of which we spoke earlier. The universities, which claim universality and to take all knowledge for their province, are narrowly and provincially western. By the classics are meant Greek and Latin, and by philosophy only the West. While scientists who may be disturbed at their separation from the arts rarely imagine those to be any other than European arts. The great masterpieces of Indian and Chinese, Persian and Japanese, painting and sculpture, so often religious in inspiration, are known to many of the general public but little in universities and art schools.

Yet the religious classics of Asia are as important to interracial understanding as are the Bible and Shakespeare to a knowledge of England. The Gītā is recited daily by countless Hindus, the Qur'ān by millions of Arabs, the Dhammapada by all Buddhists, the Tao Tê Ching by numberless Chinese. Yet these very names are almost unknown to many leaders of western thought and government. Could there be a more striking instance of western ignorance and arrogance?

These religions and their classics are the binding power of their communities. We may devote a great deal of time and energy to improving communications, raising the standard of living, developing industry, but these alone will not make 'one world' in any more than a geographical sense. The problem of today is how to avoid quarrels and wars, and turn world society into world community. The construction of a world-wide harmony is too great a task to be undertaken except with religious faith. For the necessary energy, vision and goodwill are available from no other source.

Rather then than look upon religion as 'shackles of the past' which Hindus or Muslims will leave behind as soon as they are industrialized, it is vitally important that the great role of religion in human affairs should be recognized. 'Man does not live by bread alone', and man's faith is a potent and incalculable factor in all he does. Governments should at least encourage the study of religions, so that their resources may be understood and drawn upon for building harmony and peace. And since governments subsidize universities to such a large extent they might see to it that religions are studied there.

Mention has been made of the small place that comparative religion is given in English universities. The two oldest, with their vast resources and foundations make but a tiny contribution, little enough at Oxford and nothing at all at Cambridge. Many of the modern universities, though not all the latest of them, have established small departments of theology. But they have not been clear what to do with them, and they are almost all exclusively concerned with Christian and in effect Protestant theology. Theology is suspect already of a bias in favour of Christian dogma, and this adds to the suspicion that merely the training of the Christian ministry is being effected, in the narrowest manner. Even in Manchester and London, where there is greater scope and other religions are studied, it is almost assumed that this must be from the Christian point of view only. At any rate it is virtually impossible for a Jew or a Hindu to study for a theological degree, or to pursue research for a higher degree, without having gone through the mill of study for a Christian degree, with New Testament Greek and church history.

It may be suggested that the newer universities should take a broader view and establish chairs or departments which take all religions for their province, with the necessary specialists in different fields serving in a common department. Where possible at least some of those teaching the facts of other religions should be members of those religions themselves, so that the faith can be presented from the inside and depreciation from the outside avoided. This is not always possible, and academic standards in some eastern countries are often not what are required here. At least it should be recognized that the teacher of another religion needs to keep in close and constant touch with the country where it flourishes. So Cantwell Smith says, 'It is coming to be recognized that part of the cost of setting up a department of Oriental studies in a Western university is the provision of travel funds and of arrangements for what is unfortunately still called "leave", for the staff, who must have access to the Orient just as much as a chemistry professor must have access to a chemistry laboratory.'[2]

While there should not be a Christian 'bias' in comparative religion, or any academic theology, that does not mean to say that one must be an agnostic to study it. Not so long ago it was thought in universities that to be impartial or scientific one should not be 'engaged' in the study; this is hardly possible in any branch of learning, and certainly not in religion. One who has no religion is likely to oppose religion, to seek to debunk it, or to be sceptical of its claims. So today it is more common to claim that only those who have a religious faith can understand the faith of others. This is particularly important between religions. For while no doubt only the Muslim understands Islam fully, yet the Christian more than the unbeliever can understand and expound the emphasis on the unity of God or the devotions of the Sūfī.

The best non-Muslim scholars have tried to expound Islam in a way that is meaningful to a Western audience and also that does justice to the faith of Islam. Arabs have not yet succeeded in expounding their faith to us sufficiently well for us to feel its strength, and herein lies part of our underestimate of the Arab world. On the other hand they may well be dissatisfied with our presentations unless they feel they are true, fair, and perceptive. 'Anything that I say about Islam as a living faith is valid only in so far as Muslims can say "amen" to it.' So Cantwell Smith indicates the task of the teacher of comparative religion in a modern university. 'The task of a non-Muslim scholar writing about Islam

[2] *Comparative Religion: Whither—and Why?* p. 32n.

is that of constructing an exposition that will do justice to the faith in men's hearts by commanding their assent once it is formulated. It is a creative task and a challenging one.'[3]

In the past the comparative study of religions has often tended to be equated with the history of religion. And it is true that the history of religions is important for an understanding of them. At the beginning of this century, when the faculty of the history of religions was being opened in the university of Berlin, the great church historian Adolf Harnack said, 'it needs but little consideration to recognize that the study of each single religion ought by no means to be separated from the study of the *history* of the people concerned . . . To try to study the religion alone is a more childish undertaking than to examine only the roots or the blossoms instead of the whole plant.'

Unfortunately this seemed to give a pigeonhole into which comparative religion could conveniently be dropped. It was part of history, or even archaeology. This made it an academic study, it was dead and divorced from those trying questions of comparison which led only to the expression of prejudice. But simply as history this approach to comparative religion ran into a number of difficulties.

There was first the question as to how far the different religions had a history. It was easy enough with Islam and Christianity, which sprang as reforms from religions already established or 'in the full light of history'. It was a little harder with Buddhism, whose early centuries are known only from oral tradition and legend. But Indian, and to a large extent Chinese, religion goes back to time immemorial. The Aryans entered India somewhere round about 1500 B.C. and their Vedic oral 'scriptures' seemed to give the beginnings or the first clear formulations of Brahmanism. But the discovery of the remains of the Indus civilization in the 1920's, a culture which the Aryans destroyed but which left traces and inscriptions, still undeciphered today, posed anew the still unsolved problems of the origins and character of Hinduism.

Behind all this there was the question of the beginnings

[3] *ibid.*, p. 44.

of the history of all religion. Many studies of the history of religion about the turn of this century began with chapters on the Origins and Nature of Religion. These questions are exceedingly difficult to answer, and the historian has to hand over to the prehistorian and the archaeologist, for it seems that traces of religion are found hundreds of thousands of years back. The latest summary of the position was given by E. O. James in his *Prehistoric Religion* (1957), and he was carefully reserved on the questions of the beginning of religion, and whether and how far early men had a conception of a supreme spirit or spirits.

All this was prehistory, and not clearly relevant to modern religions. Though it used to be assumed that the modern illiterates of Africa, Australia and other remote parts were 'primitive', in the sense that they retained ancient beliefs and customs almost unchanged and so could tell us what our own remote ancestors were like. There was little evidence for this assumption, for all peoples have a history, even if it is unwritten, and have developed along their own lines, or even have fallen away from some previous higher culture of which there are many examples. The Freudian assumption of religion emanating from some supposed Oedipus complex was even more baseless; rarely can such a popular theory have been erected upon such a lack of historical evidence. Freud's study of Moses and monotheism is another example of a great mind making howlers in a strange field of study, for no serious Old Testament scholar accepts his fantasy.

A further disadvantage of the history of religious approach was that it dealt with the externals of religion almost exclusively. This was inevitable since it was concerned with the past. But history occupied the field to the neglect of the living religion: *The History of Buddhist Thought; Confucius, the Man and the Myth*, and so on, these were invaluable studies, but they did not tell us what it is like to be a Buddhist or a Confucian today.

A great deal of excellent work has been done by the history of religions schools, and their work was summed up in the monumental twelve-volume *Encyclopaedia of Religion and Ethics*, compiled over the years 1908 to 1921, and reprinted since. This is still a treasure house of information, though much of it is even now becoming dated, especially the articles on 'primitive' religions. It is parallel to the great series of *Sacred Books of the East,* now all out of print but giving translations of many eastern religious classics, many of which have not yet been replaced. These provided the standards for the popular smaller editions of oriental classics of which we have spoken and which are now so easily available.

In a sense the work of the history school has been done, or at least the first stage has been completed, though new work is constantly under way, particularly on the continent and in America. But the history and the externals of religion have been well studied. The task today, with this fine and sure foundation is to go on to study what are now called significantly 'living religions'. Two fine American studies of world religions, and called *The Religions of Man* and *Man's Religions,*[4] are typical of the new approach.

It is interesting that the comparative study of religion has been taken up by sociologists and anthropologists. A number of university departments of these disciplines include a course on comparative religion, while their neighbouring theological departments usually neglect it. The anthropologists have recognized the importance of religion in 'primitive' society, and in many studies of field work in Africa and elsewhere religion plays a prominent part.

The sociologists and anthropologists treat religion as a living thing. They are concerned with it as a function of society and try to estimate its place and importance. From Sir James Frazer onwards they have sought to explain religion, and sometimes to explain it away. But they observed it, in its outward forms and rituals, and tried to define its social function.

Differently from the historians of religion these field workers have been unconcerned with history and the development of ideas and have concentrated on living religion. They might have said to Harnack that the historians had concentrated on the roots and neglected the flower, though

[4] 1958 and 1949.

they would come under his strictures for studying the flower without reference to the plant. Of great influence in modern studies was Radcliffe-Brown. He considered the study of beliefs and the history of doctrine to have distorted the true perspective of religious study, and insisted on the approach through ritual. 'To understand a particular religion we must study its effects. The religion must therefore be studied in *action* . . . We must first of all examine the specifically religious actions, the ceremonies and the collective or individual rites.'[5]

So the anthropologists carefully observed rites, even took part in sacrifices, and compiled masses of notes on their observations. But of course they never believed in the religions they studied. As Raymond Firth says, they took up an As-If attitude. In fact most of them were atheists, or at least agnostics, and had no religious beliefs of their own. So it was a study of externals, or of delusions at best.

The anthropologists studied the religions of 'primitive' or illiterate peoples. And very few sociologists indeed ventured to tackle the great historical and scriptural religions. Max Weber was an outstanding exception, but his studies of Chinese and Indian religion deal expertly with the Confucian bureaucracy, the caste-system, and the like, but are quite unsatisfactory on the history or the doctrines of the religions. The nervousness of others is also understandable, for the major religions are vast systems, with almost unlimited scriptures and infinite variety of beliefs. How could an unbeliever, even given the time and equipment, be expected to appreciate the importance of the debates on the relationship of Brahman and ātman, or the significance of the long Sūfī quest for union with God?

In stressing that religion must be studied in action, that it is controlled by sentiments, and that rite and worship express these, the anthropologists have done a great service. But their progress has been checked because they have stopped at these externals. They have taken the observable signs of the religion as if they were the religion itself. But religion is a concern of persons, it can only be explained by

[5] *Structure and Function in Primitive Society*, (1952), p. 177.

persons who hold it, or inferred by those who hold a like faith.

So it is that whereas in the early years of this century it was often assumed that a detached scholar needed to be a secular rationalist, in recent years some of the best studies of other religions have been made by Christians, and they are being joined by committed members of other faiths who are learning to make scholarly expositions of their own religion that are comprehensible to the West.

Finally, the philosophers of religion can play a great role in helping to bridge the gap between East and West. This was more clearly apparent fifty years ago, when Idealism was still dominant in European philosophy and it seemed that it had affinities with the Vedāntic philosophy of India, in its search for the underlying unity of all things. But later trends in European thought, positivism and linguistic analysis, have seemed to deny all possibility of expressing metaphysics in a meaningful way. Perhaps this phase is passing, but leaving a legacy of care in the use of words. The modern caution observable in making statements about ultimate reality or the immortality of the soul, is comparable in some ways to the Buddhist reluctance to speculate about such things. Yet the most traditional Buddhist believes firmly in a spiritual way, even when the goal may not be defined in positive terms. Hinduism is nearer to Christianity, and Islam nearer still, but their philosophies need study in the West, and by the West, and by professional philosophers, not just by Indologists and Arabists. Western thought has already been widely studied in the East, and deeper communication is necessary on both sides.[6]

When statements are made about another religion they must be recognized as fair within the context of that religion. This applies to statements made from any religious, and even more from an agnostic, position. So it has been said that '*it is the business of comparative religion to construct statements about religion that are intelligible within*

[6] I am grateful to Professor H. D. Lewis for suggestions on this and several other points.

at least two traditions simultaneously.'[7]

The academic study of religions must be acceptable within three traditions: the academic, the Christian and the Muslim, Hindu, or Buddhist, or whatever the field of study may be. Fresh light on old problems and removal of centuries of misunderstanding will come when, say, a Christian and a Muslim can together produce a study of some Christian or Muslim doctrine or practice. Only in this way will other faiths be understood seriously and from within. For it is often felt that European scholarship, with its emphasis on classification and system, studies merely the externals.

Acknowledgement must be made of the great work of Western Orientalists during the last hundred years or so. It is they who opened up the East not only to the West, but also to itself. The French Orientalist Sylvain Lévi brought this out most clearly when he said, 'By an anomaly without parallel among the rest of mankind it is by teachings from abroad that she (i.e. India) has begun to know her true greatness'. The Buddha, who is now being hailed as the greatest of all Indians, had almost been forgotten in the land of his birth till modern times. Ashoka, greatest of emperors, had disappeared from view till 1830 when the Englishman Prinsep and other scholars deciphered the inscriptions on the pillars and rocks that Ashoka had left but nobody could read. Sanskrit was unknown to most Indians and the Vedas inaccessible to all but the few until our day. So Lévi concludes, 'It is Europe who has given back Buddha and Ashoka to India.'[8]

But scholarship alone is not enough, and there is a kind of dry-as-dust approach to comparative religion which would dissect and label it, but miss the living organisms. There are severe limitations to a detached, almost agnostic, scientific attitude. Valuable as it may be when studying dead remains and archaeological treasures, it soon loses its grip when faced with a living faith. Even the texts of the past are revered and recited today and taken as guides to conduct. Involvement is necessary in religious study, and men

[7] *Comparative Religion: Whither—and Why?*, p. 52 (author's italics).
[8] *L'Inde et le Monde*, p. 15.

who try to understand another religion must both know what it means to have a faith, and also be prepared to meet men of different faith on equal terms.

Professor C. J. Bleeker has pointed out that Indian and Chinese scholars approach the comparative study of religions in a different way from those most common in the West. The best of them are just as scholarly and they like to speak of the 'science of religion', rather than comparative religion or the history of religion. But this is because they are usually dealing with the living religions, and not those of the past that so often fascinate Westerners with their bent for the antique. And Easterners are concerned with gaining a deeper insight into the value of religion, in which intuition as well as ratiocination is needed.

Hendrik Kraemer speaks of the 'coming dialogue' of religions, as if despite all the contacts of East and West the issues are not yet joined. He recognizes that there is a great deal of dialogue on the borderline, or 'dialogue of inexperts', but he insists that now the time has come for theologians to take other theologies seriously. While we differ from him profoundly on the theological standpoint, yet we are glad to agree wholeheartedly that theologians must wake up to the importance of the changed position of today. The comparative study of religions must no longer be regarded as a queer option, for those whose taste takes them that way. 'We have got beyond the time when a Chair for the History of Religions in a Theological Faculty was sufficient to do justice to the new religious worlds which are interpreted by scientific inquisitiveness.'[9]

All theological thinkers must now reckon with the new worlds that have opened up. In the same way that religious thinkers have struggled with the claims of science, and the scientific world-view, so they must now recognize the impingement of that other great thought-world, the religions of Asia, and produce 'an apologetic arising out of a sincere and open dialogue with the non-Christian religions'. This is important not only for academic reasons but also for pastoral needs, for the lay 'inexperts' are often in the thick of discussion with the vast amount of Eastern ideological

[9] *World Cultures and World Religions*, p. 365.

'invasion' of a West that is in many ways ready to be invaded. Not only do they want guidance about avatars and *nirvāna*, but they need to see their own leaders tackling these problems.

In non-academic circles the confrontation and dialogue of religions proceeds, as ever more contacts are made between East and West. As the common man has benefited from the labours of specialists in the history and languages of religion, so he should from all future ventures. As more directly involved, often, it is the more important for the layman to be fair and sympathetic in his study and show that religion can be a uniting rather than a devisive force.

The progress made so far by students of comparative religion, and the goal to be aimed at, may best be summed up in the words of Professor Cantwell Smith: 'The traditional form of Western scholarship in the study of other men's religions was that of an impersonal presentation of an "it". The first great innovation in recent times has been the personalization of the faiths observed, so that one finds a discussion of a "they". Presently the observer becomes personally involved, so that the situation is one of a "we" talking about a "they". The next step is a dialogue, where "we" talk to "you". If there is listening and mutuality, this may become that "we" talk *with* "you". The culmination of this progress is when "we all" are talking with each other about "us".'[10]

[10] *Comparative Religion: Whither—and Why?*, p. 34.

INDEX